D1033948

No Safety in Numbers

How the Computer quantified everything and made people risk-aversive

The Hampton Press Communication Series
Media Ecology

Lance Strate, supervisory editor

No Safety in Numbers

How the Computer quantified everything and made people risk-aversive

Henry J. Perkinson
New York University

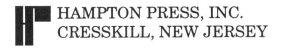

HAMPTON PRESS, INC.
CRESSKILL, NEW JERSEY

QA
76.9
.C66
P465
1996

Copyright © 1996 by Hampton Press, Inc.

All rights reserved. No part of this publication may be reproduced, stored in a retrieval system, or transmitted in any form or by any means, electronic, mechanical, photocopying, microfilming, recording, or otherwise, without permission of the publisher.

Printed in Canada

Library of Congress Cataloging-in-Publication Data

Perkinson, Henry J.
    No safety in numbers : how the computer quantified everything and made people risk aversive / Henry J. Perkinson
       p. cm. -- (The Hampton Press communication series. Media ecology)
    Includes bibliographical references and index.
    ISBN 1-57273-062-5 (cloth). -- ISBN 1-57273-063-3 (pbk.)
    1. Computers and civilization. 2. Computers--Social aspects.
3. Risk communication. 4. Risk perception. I. Title. II. Series.
QA76.9.C66P465 1996
303.48'34--dc20   96-21832
                                                  CIP

Hampton Press, Inc.
23 Broadway
Cresskill, NJ 07626

*For Audrey: incomparable editor,
best friend, and beloved wife.*

*I also want to thank my children, Amelie, Anthea, Sam,
for their help; and Aleta and Ariel, for being there.*

CONTENTS

INTRODUCTION

This is not a book about computers. It is a book about the effects of the computer on culture. Electronic computers have been around ever since World War II, but only in the 1980s did the technology develop to a point at which they could be mass produced and used everywhere.

As a result of its mass production the computer has become a dominant medium of communication. By this I mean that it defines the culture. Every medium of communication has a structure that allows us to store, retrieve, transmit, and process information. Most of this information is about culture—our arrangements, institutions, practices, ideas, values, and beliefs. Yet, media of communication do more than serve as vehicles for information and culture; they actually make the culture what it is. Thus, we say that media of communication form, or inform, the culture. Scholars often describe a given culture by reference to its dominant, or defining, medium of communication. When, for example, speech is the sole or main means of communication, we call it an oral culture. If writing becomes the dominant medium, we call it a literate culture. Historically, the dominant media of communication have been speech, writing, print, television, and the computer. The last two dominant media, both of which appeared in the second half of the 20th century, are electronic media, so our present age is frequently spoken of as an electronic culture.

1

How do dominant media define a culture?

The structure of a medium—which allows us to store, retrieve, transmit, and process information—provides access to information and control over it. The dominant media of communication in any age determine the amount of control over information, and the degree of accessibility to information. By doing so, they define or form the cultural arrangements, including the policies, practices, procedures, beliefs, values, and attitudes common to that culture. In many respects an electronic culture resembles an oral culture, as can be seen by comparing both of these with a literate culture.

In literate cultures (whether based on writing or print) information is easily controlled and access to it limited. Only those who are literate have access to information, and those who own the printing presses, or oversee them, have control over information. As a result, social, political, and economic arrangements are more hierarchical than in an oral culture or in an electronic culture, in which the control of information is more difficult and accessibility to information easier to come by. In an oral culture, whoever can speak and listen has access to information, whereas in an electronic culture, whoever has a television set or a computer has access to information. As a result, the cultural arrangements in oral and electronic cultures are not hierarchical, but rather take on a network kind of structure, are more egalitarian, and, in the case of an electronic culture, more pluralistic.

Second, a literate culture has more competition—social, political, and economic—than an oral or electronic culture because in a literate culture information is more scarce, not widely or collectively shared. In both oral and electronic cultures there is an abundance of information. So, because it is possible to share information in these kinds of cultures, cooperation, not competition becomes the ideal and the norm. In both oral and electronic cultures people believe that the relationships and interactions that take place in the economic, political, and social spheres should be collaborative and collective.

Third, a literate culture is more individualistic insofar as the people in it hold that a person's place in the social, political, and economic order depends upon him-or herself. This is because when there is strong control over information and accessibility is limited, only those who have the ability and talent and put forth the effort will be able to acquire information. But when information is more accessible and shared, as in an oral culture, a person's place or condition is held to be the outcome of luck, or the work of the gods; whereas in an electronic culture when information is also accessible and shared, each person regards his or her position in the society as the result of a myriad of factors over which one has no control. In an electronic culture it is the society or the "system" that determines one's place or condition.

Finally, in a literate culture, the goings-on in the universe are held to be rational, or they happen in accord with rational laws or principles known to experts. In a literate culture, people view such knowledge as objective, true, and authoritative. The construction of this rational, objective knowledge (science) is the work of the experts themselves, who, of course, have privileged access to and control over such information. But in an oral culture in which no such privileged access or control exists, there are no knowledge experts, and the goings-on in the universe are held to be the doings of the gods, whose subjective purposes are usually unfathomable—although shamans and oracles can divine them. An electronic culture, on the other hand, provides almost limitless access to all kinds of information, undermining all controls, and thereby destroys the monopoly of experts. In an electronic culture, the goings-on in the universe are explainable in a wide variety of ways, but no explanation is authoritative. Each is simply construed as a perspective, a point of view, no more correct or true than any other point of view. In an electronic culture people deny the possibility of objective knowledge and construe all knowledge as the subjective beliefs of different groups, each of whom seeks to control other people and events.

In two previous books on the history of media in western culture I argued that the dominant media of communication have facilitated cultural progress—especially during the time when each medium first appeared. Progress occurred because the then-existing culture was encoded in the new medium—in speech, in writing, in print, or on television—which thereby enabled people at that time to view their culture in new ways, allowing them to uncover inadequacies, weaknesses, and insufficiencies not apparent heretofore. This led people to make dramatic changes in the culture.

In *How Things Got Better* (1995), I attempted to show how the emergence of speech enabled human beings to create a human culture composed of social, political, and economic arrangements and institutions, as well as new intellectual understandings of the world they inhabited. Writing, when it first appeared, enabled people to create civilizations with elaborate and far-reaching collectivized and cooperative arrangements hierarchically organized in political, social, and economic institutions held together through subjective loyalties. The arrival of the printing press in the late 15 century enabled people to construct a modern world, based on modern science, composed of constitutional polities, capitalist economies, and open societies. In the modern world the values of equality replaced hierarchy, collectivism gave way to individualism, competition pushed out cooperation, and objectivity triumphed over subjectivism.

In *Getting Better: The Moral Effects of Television* (1991), I tried to show how television helped uncover some of the moral inadequacies in modern culture: the unfair, discriminatory, and unjust relations that inhered in modern social, political, and economic institutions. Television also helped reveal some of the immoral consequences of modern science. In that book I claimed that we are in the throes, once again, of radically transforming our culture. I suggested that the new culture might be a synthesis of the values of modern culture with those of premodern culture, thereby creating a postmodern culture. This new culture would combine the values of hierarchy with equality, competition with cooperation, individualism with collectivism, and objectivity with subjectivity.

This present book is an update on that emerging postmodern culture. It is less optimistic than the previous books because, although I do see clear evidence that things are getting better, I also fear that in our current postmodern world we are too much influenced by the values promoted by an electronic culture. Today we witness the breakdown of hierarchies, the decline of competition, the eclipse of individualism, and the demise of objective rational knowledge. In place of these we see emerging the characteristics of an electronic culture: demands for equality, pleas for cooperation, praise for collectivism, and the rise of subjectivism.

The first dominant electronic medium, television, helped us uncover the moral inadequacies of modern culture—the culture that the printing press had helped us create. To reduce these moral inadequacies we have made sweeping changes in our social, political, and economic arrangements, thereby inaugurating a postmodern culture. The second dominant electronic medium, the computer, has enabled us to recognize the risks inherent in modern culture.

How has the computer made us more risk aversive?

Many a commentator has noted that the electronic computer can store more information, retrieve it faster, process it more accurately, and transmit it more widely than was ever possible before. Computers have enabled us to accomplish tasks with more ease, speed, and efficiency. Computers, they tell us, have reduced time and overcome space: We now can perform a multiplicity of transactions at a distance and with the speed of light. All this is true. Yet, I think that the most profound impact of computerization is the mathematization of our culture.

We can describe culture and explain human goings on in three ways: by means of language, by pictures, or by mathematics. We have used language and pictures since prehistoric times, but, until recently, few, except for some social scientists, have used mathematics for this purpose. But, as a result of the proliferation of computers in the last decades, it has become more common to encode culture in statistics, in algorithmic programs, and in linear and nonlinear equations—all of which gives us new ways of looking at our culture.

The computer converts facts into statistics; it transforms procedures into processes; and it translates problems into equations. Through computerization the facts of the social, political, and economic worlds have been converted into data, which means that each fact now becomes part of a pattern, or a trend, often not discernible heretofore. When computers are employed to perform tasks formerly done by human beings, this transforms human designed "procedures" into mathematical "processes": The procedures, that is, the transactions, operations, and functions—that human beings formerly carried out routinely, properly, steadily, and more or less correctly, are now programmed into regularized, automatic, "processes" that are errorless. And with the coming of the computer, problems that crop up in the political, economic, and social spheres are now simulated, or modeled, on the computer in the form of linear and nonlinear equations.

All of these applications of the computer—the conversion of facts into statistical data, the transformation of procedures into processes, and the conversion of problems into equations—have generated new information about our social, political, and economic arrangements. This increase in information brings with it a deeper appreciation of the complexity of these worlds. Yet, not only is our culture more complex than ever before imagined, it is fraught with risks never before recognized.

By encoding the culture in mathematics the computer has revealed that in this society we are all less protected than we believed ourselves to be. By quantifying the goings-on in our culture and presenting them in statistics plotted on charts, graphs, and tables, the computer has revealed that we are all threatened by heretofore unrecognized risks to our health, safety, and well-being.

Thus, in spite of the fantastic improvements in medicine and health care that have taken place in the modern era, we now witness daily ever rising fears about sickness and disease and ever deepening concern about physical fitness and diet. And, although a smaller percentage of people suffer accidents than have in the past, we find ourselves more worried about safety and threats to our well-being. We worry not only about ourselves, but about the planet, too: We fear that it is also at risk—from pollution and from depletion of its resources. In Part Two, I argue that the computer has brought about these risk aversions.

In the economic sphere capitalism has clearly emerged triumphant, and the computer has certainly played a role in promoting economic growth. But, at the same time, as I argue in Part Three, the computer has caused massive job dislocations. This has generated widespread risk aversion among employees in all occupations and at all levels of expertise. This risk aversion has manifested itself in demands for protectionist policies, in growing anti-immigrant sentiments, and in calls for more government regulation of business, industry, and finance.

As I argue in Part Four in the political sphere the computer, has created a crisis of democracy. The increasing number of polls and surveys made possible by the computer have made political leaders more aware of the needs and concerns of their constituents. But instead of producing better government this computer-generated information has converted politicians into permanent candidates who avoid any pronouncement, any decision, any vote that would put their reelection at risk.

Finally, I offer a cautionary word about my analysis. I reject so-called technological or media determinism. I believe that people—not media—determine the course of events. We do this by trying to solve problems—or better, we do this by trying to eliminate inadequacies, bads, evils, mistakes, and errors when these are uncovered. We ascertain inadequacies and mistakes by means of the intellectual frameworks we carry around in our heads. As I see it, it is our intellectual frameworks—our set of beliefs about how the world works—that are the motor force of history. In Part One I argue that the computer has played a crucial role in transforming the intellectual outlook that underlies the increase in risk aversion to the mathematicized culture the computer has created.

Risk aversion has brought about radical changes in our political, social, and economic arrangements. These dramatic and sweeping changes have undoubtedly made things better. But they have also brought about new cultural crises: Our society has become more unstable, our economic growth has faltered, and our polity has become less governable.

PART ONE

A RISK-FREE INTELLECTUAL WORLD

1

MATHEMATICS AND HUMAN KNOWLEDGE

Since the late 1960s, the intellectual world seems to have turned upside down. Not the natural sciences, but the humanities and some of the social sciences now put forth points of view almost exactly opposite to the views they traditionally presented. The intellectual world has changed, changed utterly.

Philosophers tell us there is no truth; literary scholars announce that there are no texts, and no authors, either. Anthropologists declare there are no primitive societies, and historians insist there is no objective past (see Geertz, 1973, 1983; Handlin, 1979; Kernan, 1990; Rorty, 1979, 1982, 1991). Scholars seem no longer engaged in the pursuit of truth but rather occupy themselves with a quest for meaning. And the meaning each scholar comes up with is his or her own meaning. Meaning is relative: the scholar makes meaning, he or she does not discover it. With relativism comes the abandonment of objectivity, the standard hallmark of scholarship:

- Choosing between Pearl Buck and Virginia Woolf, Professor Houston Baker of the University of Pennsylvania informs us, "is no different from choosing between a hoagie and a pizza."
- Mickey Mouse may, in fact, be more important in understanding the 1930s than Franklin Roosevelt, according to one historian.

9

- "Does might make right? In a sense, the answer I must give is yes, since in the absence of a perspective independent of interpretation, some interpretive perspective will always rule by virtue of having won out over its competitors"; thus, Stanley Fish, Arts and Science Professor of English, Professor of Law, and Chair of the Department of English at Duke University.
- "I (Joanna Overing, Senior Lecturer in the Social Anthropology of Latin America, London School of Economics), for one, consider it unthinkable to claim that a Piaroa of the Venezuelan rain forest is irrational when he says that rain is the urine of the deity, Ofo Da'a."

Many are the theories put forth to explain this revolution in the humanities and the social sciences. One explanation blames academic specialization. As more and more is published in the various fields, each scholar must try to find a new angle, a new facet, a new interpretation, in order to get into print. Over time, the new angles, the new interpretations have become more narrow and more esoteric. Here, the specialization explanation shades into the professionalization explanation: to secure promotions and tenure, professors must publish—it matters little what they publish, they simply must publish. Yet, this intellectual revolution now afoot comprises more than simply the micro-specializations of young professors trying to climb the slippery slope of academia. This academic specialization theory does not explain the blatant repudiation of objectivity and the embracing of subjectivity by scholars in the humanities and social sciences. Objectivity—disinterested scholarship—is something these scholars ridicule as a mask that hides the "fact" that all scholarship is value-laden and thus an instrument to impose values on others. What matters most to these scholars is not so-called "objectivity" but rather that scholarship manifests the correct values, that is, progressive values.

This outlook of politically correct values is promoted by those identified as "tenured radicals," most of whom were former student activists in the late 1960s, who since then have moved on in the long march through the universities to become professors in the humanities and the social sciences. Richard Grenier (1991) suggests that they are following the teachings of Antonio Gramsci, the Italian Marxist, who argued that it is useless to try to change society without first changing human consciousness. Critics like Roger Kimball (1990) and Charles Sykes (1990, 1992) see these tenured radicals employing their academic fields to combat sexism, racism, capitalism, and elitism in all their guises. But in launching this war against western culture, they are, as Peter Shaw (1989) points out, waging a war against the intellect by destroying the values, methods, and goals of traditional scholarship.

Finally, there is the explanation put forth by Allan Bloom in his best selling book, *The Closing of the American Mind* (1987), which lays the present intellectual situation on the head of Nietzsche, whose nihilism has penetrated the minds of American scholars and become the source for the epistemological and cultural relativism they now proclaim.

In Part One, I want to suggest that the intellectual revolution that has taken place in the humanities and the social sciences can best be explained as an instance of risk-aversion brought about by the electronic computer. I make no attempt to refute the alternate explanations mentioned above, because I do believe that they can be subsumed under my risk aversion explanation.

What risks were the humanists and social scientist scholars trying to avert? Simply put, it was the threat of the scientization of their fields. In trying to avert this, they turned their fields upside down.

Ever since modern science first emerged, it has put itself forward as the paradigm of knowledge. As a result, the humanists, initially, and later the social scientists, have had difficulty in establishing themselves as cognitive disciplines, as fields of true knowledge. With the coming of the computer some humanists and social scientists saw the opportunity to establish their fields as real cognitive disciplines. The computer, they thought, would allow them to mathematize their fields and thereby convert them into sciences. These efforts to mathematize the humanities and the social sciences led, in turn, to a counter movement against science, a movement that launched a searching reappraisal of the condition of knowledge itself. The upshot of this counter movement is the contention by many scholars today that all knowledge is subjective, relative, and without foundation—thus creating what I call a risk-free intellectual world.

THE MATHEMATIZATION OF KNOWLEDGE: A BRIEF HISTORICAL SURVEY

The antagonism between science and the humanities goes back to Greek antiquity when Plato (427-347 B.C.) first pointed out the difference between true knowledge (*scientia*) and mere opinion (*doxa*). This distinction centered on the question of how best to educate future leaders of the state. Plato insisted that nothing less than *sci-*

entia would do: We can only have just rulers, he argued, when those rulers really know what justice is; that is when they have true knowledge (*scientia*) of justice. But his arch rival Isocrates (436-338 B.C.), a teacher of rhetoric, doubted that such knowledge could be taught and opted instead for what he called "right opinion"—the wisdom contained in the traditional culture *(Paideia)* embodied in history, poetry, oratory, and drama. He argued that initiation into one's culture, into the record of the best that has been said and done, would provide future leaders with the beliefs, ideas, values, understandings, and dispositions that would intimate how one should conduct oneself as a leader. In short, the study of the humanities would initiate future leaders into their culture, which would provide intimations of how they should lead (see Bolgar, 1964; Marrou, 1956).

In the history of western education, Isocrates won out over Plato, and as a result the humanities (not philosophy) remained the central core of education from the 4th-century B.C. until the 20th century. (There was a small blip when the rediscovery of the works of Aristotle in the late 12th-century resulted in the triumph of scholasticism in the universities. This lasted until philosophy was challenged and ultimately put to rout by the rebirth [renaissance] of the humanities in the late 14th-century.)

But in the 20th century, Plato's argument that leaders should act on the basis of true knowledge (*scientia*) once again came to the fore. However, true knowledge, it was now claimed, was to be found not in the speculations of philosophy, but in science. The spectacular success of modern science in explaining phenomena encouraged the practitioners of all branches of knowledge to adopt the methods of science. With a scientific understanding of all the goings-on in the world, the argument now went, leaders would be better able to make correct decisions

Modern science first emerged in the 17th century when Francis Bacon (1561-1626) urged people to turn away from reading books to read instead the book of nature. Science, by which Bacon meant the careful, direct observation of the world, would, he promised, provide us with true knowledge. Armed with true knowledge, we could improve the human estate, better our quality of life, and improve life chances for all.

Although Bacon is sometimes lauded as the father of modern science, he merely provided the vision, not the method. It was Galileo Galilei (1564-1642) who recognized that the book of nature is written in mathematical notation ("Il libro della nature e scritto in lingua matematica.") It was he and his fellow physicists of the 17th century who launched modern science by providing mathematical explanations of how the world works.

Yet, although Galileo is accepted as the true founder of modern science, it was not he but the French philosopher, Rene Descartes (1596-1650) who created the first modern philosophy of nature. Descartes, a pure mathematician (unlike Galileo who was primarily an applied mathematician), constructed a new picture of the world set in a mathematical framework. Descartes explained all of the phenomena of nature in terms of particles—their magnitude, their motions, and the figures they composed.

Unable to break completely with the past, Descartes left two substances outside the mathematical order of nature: God and the human soul. It was left to his followers, Benedict Spinoza (1632-77) and Thomas Hobbes (1588-1679), to incorporate them as well.

God, Spinoza explained, is the mathematical order itself. God is not an anthropomorphic being: He has no intellect, nor will. God is the logical mathematical order of nature, perfect and divine.

Hobbes overcame the reluctance of Descartes to draw the logical conclusion that in a mathematical universe man must be a completely material being whose "mind" is nothing but "the motions in certain parts of an organic body." Reasoning, Hobbes explained, is essentially computation.

While philosophers like Spinoza and Hobbes were carrying forward Descartes' dream of a mathematical philosophy of nature, the mathematical approach made great strides in the nonmechanical sciences. Robert Boyle (1627-91), the father of modern chemistry, shared the notion that mathematical principles are "the alphabet in which God wrote the world." Adopting the atomistic approach of Descartes, Boyle explained the action of gas under pressure as the movement of minute bodies that he called corpuscles. Boyle's Law supplies the precise mathematical formulation of the relationship between volume and pressure (under a constant pressure). During the 17th-century, others, such as Mariotte, Toricelli, and Blaise Pascal, continued to develop mathematical measurements of the pressure and density of fluids and gases. Hales began quantitative studies in physiology, such as the measure of body temperature and blood pressure. Harvey proved by quantitative arguments that the blood pumped from the heart made a complete circuit of the body before returning to the heart. Quantitative studies took place in botany, too, when investigators determined the rate at which plants absorbed and evaporated water.

The most spectacular and most influential mathematical interpretation of nature came from Isaac Newton (1642-1727). Prior to Newton, scientists like Galileo had mathematically described motions on or near the surface of the earth. And others, like Johannes Kepler (1571-1630), had formulated mathematical laws that described the action of the sun on the planets, as well as the actions of the earth on objects near it. By fitting the findings of the astronomers and the physicists into a single mathematical system, Newton's *Principia Mathematica* demonstrated that the universe is a perpetual motion machine.

By 1789, 18 editions of the *Principia Mathematica* had appeared, along with numerous popularizations: 40 in English, 16 in French, 11 in Latin, 3 in German, and 1 each in Italian and Portuguese (Kline, 1953, p. 197). Not only were Newton's laws found to embrace an amazing variety of phenomena—light and sound, for example—but they inspired Gottfried Leibnitz (1646-1716), a philosopher-mathematician, to attempt to broaden the scope of mathematical language to devise a universal calculus that would be used to inform and prosecute all inquiries in all fields. Leibnitz's ambitious project had to await the development of symbolic logic in the late 19th century. But, in the meantime, the so-called philosophes of France during the 18th century set out to make the study of human beings and their institutions somewhat mathematical.

In these efforts, the philosophes took their lead from John Locke (1632-1704), who was neither a scientist, nor a mathematician, nor French—but an English physician turned philosopher. In his analysis of human knowledge, Locke adopted a "geometrical spirit"— at least this is what Voltaire (1694-1778), the leading light of the philosophes, argued. By imitating Locke, and adopting his "geometrical spirit," the philosophes hoped to uncover the laws that governed the social world, which would then enable enlightened rulers to replace existing irrational social institutions that generated conflict and disorder with rational institutions that would promote social and political harmony.

Perhaps the most dramatic example of this geometric spirit appeared in the mechanistic theory of human nature put forth by LaMettrie and Helvetius. As Helevitius put it: "Man is a machine which, once set in motion by physical sensibility executes all his acts necessarily."

Although later in the 18th century reaction against this mathematization of both the material and social worlds came from romantics like Baron d'Holbach (1723-89) and Johann Wolfgang von Goethe (1742-1832), the phenomenal success of quantification in the natural sciences—the work of Lavoissier in chemistry and Laplace in physics, for example—firmly established mathematics as the foundation of all true knowledge. Pierre Simon Laplace (1749-1827) utilized the calculus of probabilities to prove that the irregularities in the eccentricities of the elliptical paths of the planets were periodic, thus demonstrating that all the motions in the heavens are orderly and the universe stable. Whereas Newton had claimed that it was God who corrected the irregularities in the planets, Laplace announced: "I have no need of this hypothesis." By the end of the 18th century, few would disagree with the pronouncement of Immanuel Kant (1729-1804), *the* philosopher of the enlightenment, when he wrote: "Each natural science is real science only in so far as it is mathematical."

In the 19th century, physics became even more mathematized, with the mathematics becoming ever more esoteric and incomprehensible to most lay people. According to Morris Kline, the electromagnetic theory of James Clarke Maxwell (1831-79) consisted of a set of mathematical laws that "surpass even Newton's gravitational theory in embracing a variety of diverse phenomena: electrons, the sun, electric currents, magnetic effects, radio waves, infra-red waves, light waves, ultra-violet waves, x-rays, and gamma rays (1953, p. 316). When quantum physics emerged at the close of the century, marking the end of Newton's mechanical world system, physics became almost completely mathematized, prompting the physicist, James Jeans (1887-1946) to declare: "The Great Architect of the universe now begins to appear as a pure mathematician."

By a "pure mathematician," Jeans referred to the fact that physics had passed from a mechanist to a mathematical foundation. Whereas in classical physics, mathematics had served primarily to represent, study, and advance the mechanical analysis of phenomena, today physicists have abandoned the notion that the universe is a mechanism like a clock. For modern physicists, the mathematical account is fundamental. The essence of any modern physical theory is a body of mathematical equations.

Of the natural sciences, biology alone remained outside the sphere of mathematics. Charles Darwin (1809-82) confessed that his own "power to follow a long and purely abstract train of thought is very limited." Yet, he did admit that his theory of evolution via natural selection was "the doctrine of Malthus applied to the whole animal and vegetable kingdom"—and the doctrine (of political economy) of Thomas Malthus (1766-1834) was a mathematical formula: Population increases at an exponential rate, whereas food supply increases at a linear rate, so that competition for survival is the law of life.

The work in genetics conducted by Gregor Mendel (1822-84) in the 19th century (but only recognized in the 20th) was the first significant application of mathematics to biology. Biology was further mathematicized by the application of statistical techniques developed in the 19th century by Galton and Pearson.

Although Voltaire had called for a "geometrical spirit" in an analysis of the social world, it was not until the 19th century that this became more than a metaphor. Auguste Comte (1798-1857), a mathematician by training, invented the term *sociology* and announced that such a discipline must, like the sciences of nature, be positivistic, that is, mathematical: "It must be remembered that the true positive spirit first came forth from the pure sources of mathematical science." Encouraged by the development and applications of statistics, Comte believed that sociology would be the last discipline to reach the positive, or scientific, stage.

As the positivists saw it, all those fields that studied man and his works—history, anthropology, and psychology, as well as sociology—must jettison speculation and search out the mathematical bases of the laws that govern society, culture, and human behavior—thereby becoming social *sciences*.

During the late 19th century, historians such as Henry Thomas Buckle and J. B. Bury in England, Hippolyte Taine in France, and Karl Lamprecht in Germany, set out to turn history into a science—without too much success, however. Nevertheless, as Comte had anticipated, psychologists and sociologists employed statistical methods to organize, process, and analyze their data about human behavior and human institutions, thereby creating scientific sociology and scientific psychology. To those who doubted that mathematics could be used to describe human conduct, the American psychologist, Edward Lee Thorndike (1876-1949) retorted: "Whatever exists, exists in some quantity, and can be measured."

LOGICAL POSITIVISM AND ITS INFLUENCE

Perhaps the most important impact of the positivist outlook was on philosophy, where it resulted in what came to be called "logical positivism," and later, "logical empiricism." Fathered by the Austrian physicist, Ernst Mach (138-1916), and after World War I nurtured by a group of mathematicians, scientists, and philosophers who called themselves the Vienna Circle, Logical Positivism became a crusade to make philosophy scientific. Led by philosophers Rudolph Carnap and Moritz Schlick, and the mathematician Kurt Godel, the logical positivists held that metaphysical speculation is nonsensical; only logic (and mathematics) and scientific statements have any meaning. Logical (and mathematical) statements are tautologically true, hence meaningful; scientific statements are empirically true—that is, based on sense observation—hence they are also meaningful. The criterion for a meaningful statement, they claimed, is verifiability, that is, a meaningful statement is one that can be verified.

Although he was not officially a member of the Vienna Circle, and did not have their high regard for science, the Viennese engineer-turned-philosopher, Ludwig Wittgenstein (1889-1951), did share the logical positivists' notion that only scientific statements have meaning. In his *Tractatus Logico Philosophicus* (1922), Wittgenstein wrote:

> The correct method of philosophy should really be like this. To say nothing . . . and then, whenever someone else tries to say something metaphysical to show him that he has given no meaning to some of the signs in his sentences. (6.53)

Wittgenstein studied philosophy at Cambridge under Bertrand Russell, who earlier had co-authored, with Alfred Whitehead, *Principia Mathematica*, wherein mathematics was "reduced" to the laws of logic. Following a suggestion of Russell, Wittgenstein sought to reduce ordinary language to logical propositions by reconstructing language on a formal model, a propositional calculus that could express the *real* forms of propositions.

According to the *Tractatus*, every scientific statement or proposition is a "picture of reality." In this view, the world is composed of objects arranged as facts. A true elementary proposition ("The cat is on the mat") pictures such a fact (The cat is on the mat). This is called an *atomic fact*. A true sentence, then, has the same logical form as the form of reality; that is, objects or things in the world are related in the same way as are words in propositions.

Wittgenstein did not explain how scientific statements are verified. This became the project of the members of the Vienna Circle, who latched on to the *Tractatus* as providing the criterion for demarcating scientific statements from meaningless statements: Scientific statements must refer to what is the case; they picture reality.

With the outbreak of World War II many members of the Vienna Circle, along with other logical positivists in Europe, were forced to migrate to Great Britain; even more of them came to the United States, where they took up positions in prominent universities. In the aftermath of the war, the logical positivists and those whom they had taught came to dominate not only American philosophy, but all intellectual discussions among American academics.

2

QUANTIFICATION AND LITERACY STUDIES

After World War II many academics shared the feeling that the time was propitious for new intellectual beginnings. This prompted the holding of numerous interdisciplinary conferences and symposia in which few could match or counter the crisp arguments and the logical distinctions put forth by the logical positivists, or logical empiricists, as some now called themselves. The fact that modern science had played such a significant role in winning the war and still remained of central importance in the ensuing "cold war" considerably strengthened the claims of the logical positivists that the only real knowledge is scientific knowledge.

One interdisciplinary conference, sponsored by the Tamiment Institute in 1958, brought a classic confrontation between the logical positivist, Ernest Naegel from Columbia University, and the literary scholar, Douglas Bush from Harvard. Naegel, after noting that "the growth of scientific intelligence has helped to bring about not only improvements in the material conditions of life but also an enhancement of its quality," went on to maintain that the humanities do not provide us with any real knowledge: Knowledge is only true or false, and only propositions are true or false; therefore, if the experiences attributed to the humanities cannot be stated in propositional form, then they are not knowledge. (Blanchard, 1959, pp. 199-202)

This was a direct attack on the so-called "dual-truth" position adopted by many humanists, who claimed that there were, in addition to the truths of science, those truths obtained from the arts and the humanities. The latter were ineffable. But as Wittgenstein had written in the last section of the *Tractatus*: "Whereof we cannot speak, thereof we should be silent." And, as Ernest Naegel pointed out to a somewhat hapless Douglas Bush, there is only one kind of truth and only one reliable method for establishing claims to truth: "The contention that the humanities employ a distinctive conception of truth and represent a mode of knowledge different from scientific knowledge seem to me to be the consequences of a failure of analysis" (Blanchard, 1959, pp. 202-203).

If the humanities were not to become marginalized in academia by being deprived of full cognitive status, then, it seemed to many humanist scholars that they too had to become scientific. This meant that both literature and history, and maybe anthropology, had to follow psychology (the science of behavior) and sociology (the science of society) and become more quantitative. They had to become human sciences. The advent of the computer facilitated this scientization, or mathematization, of these fields.

THE QUANTIFICATION OF LITERARY STUDIES

If literary studies were to be quantified, then what was there that could be counted and measured? The "New Critics," who had flourished between the two world wars and who had included John Crowe Ransom, Cleanth Brooks, Allen Tate, and R. P. Blackmur, had claimed to provide a scientific approach to literature. By a close reading of the text, the New Critics attempted to analyze how the author organized and patterned the text to make a self-contained, autonomous, entity that communicated moral, aesthetic, metaphysical knowledge to the reader. This literary analysis of the New Critics rested, of course, on the doctrine of dual truth, a doctrine that the logical positivists now ruled out.

The attack of the logical positivists led some literary scholars to abandon the New Criticism and take up something called *structuralism*, which held out the promise of finally making literary studies truly scientific. Structuralism was held to be the method for understanding what makes a piece of literature work. According to structuralism, there is a structure underlying all human conduct, a structure inherent in the mental make-up of human beings. These structures, therefore, inhere in all that humans construct—in their language, their culture, and their literature.

Invented by Ferdinand Saussure in the beginning of the 20th century, as an assumption about language, successive generations of European scholars developed and applied structuralism to the study of language (linguistics), human beings (structural anthropology), and literature (poetics).

Literary structuralists, like Roman Jakobson, who had migrated to the United States, set out to discover the underlying structures of each literary genre as well as the structure underlying the literature of a particular historical period. Structuralism aimed to be more scientific than the new criticism in-so-far as it claimed to study the underlying laws that govern the relations or structures that make the literary work what it is. Whereas the New Critics had concentrated on the literary stylistics—rhythm, metre, rhyme, and so on—that the author deliberately and consciously manipulated, and which were immediately obvious to the reader, the structures that the structuralists sought to uncover were neither immediately obvious to the reader, nor consciously or deliberately employed by the author.

During the 1960s and the 1970s, some literary scholars began to use the computer to conduct stylistic and structural analyses of literature. The computer enabled scholars to recognize and specify the algorithms of style and structure for literary works, genre, and periods. With the help of computers, literary critics were soon publishing extensive quantitative analyses of paragraph lengths, sentence length, and word lengths, as well as analyses of the interrelationships among these variables in selected literary works. The computer also facilitated extensive analysis of such stylistic aspects as imagery, rhythm, word frequency, and word associations, as well as the juxtaposition, grouping, and position of words in a text. Such computer analysis proved useful in determining authorship. (One computer analysis claimed that Paul did not write 14 of the Epistles attributed to him.)

In 1966 a manual appeared called *The Computer and Literary Style*, as well as a newsletter, soon to become a journal, called *Computers and the Humanities*. The initial newsletter announced five different conferences on the use of the computer in humanist scholarship to be held in various parts of the United States. Throughout the next decade, *Computers and the Humanities* published articles that described how literary scholars were using computers not only for stylistic analyses, but also to compile concordances of the poets, variorum editions, bibliographies, and indexes. Scholars were also using computers to construct models of literary genre, and models of literary periods, as well as to test hypotheses about the structure of individual works. Computers performed with ease much of the brute labor of scholarship—information storage and retrieval, collation and analysis—but they also had an impact on scholarly thinking: Literary scholars now put aside questions that were vague and ambiguous for those that were more explicit and objective.

Although the number of computer-assisted literary analyses increased throughout the 70s and 80s (Potter, 1989), a number of literary scholars resisted such endeavors, and derided those who conducted them. Most, but not all, of those who resisted were young. As Zbigniew Brzezinski has cogently noted, during the 1960s the younger generation was the one most directly affected by the transition to the new age of technology; especially effected were those in the humanities, who felt themselves to be the victims of what he called the *technetronic revolution*. He noted that one of the common targets of the rebellious students in the late 60s was always the university computer center, which they either liberated (i.e., occupied) or destroyed (Brzezinski, 1970, p. 108).

These (mostly young) critics complained that in trying to make the study of literature scientific, structuralism and stylistics had expunged human agency from literature and made it deterministic. Since most literary scholars had gravitated toward the study of literature because it celebrated human agency and evinced originality, creativity, and unpredictability, these folks decried the scientism of the computer people because they both subverted and trivialized literature. Take J.F. Burrows's 1987 book, *Computation into Criticism*—a computer-assisted, scientific study of the novels of Jane Austen that contains 16 tables, 33 graphs, and 10 figures on 8 personal pronouns, 6 auxiliary verb forms, 5 prepositions, 3 conjunctions, the definite and indefinite articles, and 4 other words (to, that, for, and all).

If this was how the field of literary studies was going to solve its status problem as a cognitive discipline, then such stature it might gain would be worthless. Better to reject any claims to being a scientific discipline than to sink to this. Thus, the attempt to scientize literature had created its own risk: the risk of destroying literature itself. Few literary scholars wanted to avoid the threat of marginalization among academic fields by risking the death of literature itself. It was at this juncture that some literary scholars turned back to Wittgenstein for guidance; not to the Wittgenstein of the *Tractatus*, but to the later Wittgenstein—the author of *Philosophical Investigations*.

THE LATER WITTGENSTEIN

When he completed his *Tractatus*, which was published in 1921 (in German, with an English translation appearing the following year), Wittgenstein believed that he had solved all the problems of philosophy. All philosophical problems arise because "the logic of our language is misunderstood." As I noted earlier, he maintained that the correct method in philosophy was to say nothing except "what can be said", that is, propositions of natural science—which, of course, have nothing to do with philosophy—and to point out that when someone said something metaphysical (or made an ethical or an aesthetic statement) to demonstrate that "he had failed to give a meaning to certain signs in his propositions."

Having expunged ethics, aesthetics, and metaphysics from philosophy as meaningless statements (i.e., statements that could not be verified), Wittgenstein concluded that there was little left for philosophers to do, except to serve as guides to help people demarcate meaningful (scientific) discourse from meaningless discourse. He recognized, of course, that what he had written in the *Tractatus* was not science, and, therefore, meaningless. But he thought that it served the purpose he had set out to accomplish, as he explained in the penultimate aphorism of the book:

> My propositions serve as elucidation in the following way: anyone who understands me eventually recognizes them as nonsensical, [i.e., not scientific] when he has used them. (He must, so to speak, throw away the ladder after he has climbed it.) He must transcend these propositions and he will see the world aright. (6.54)

To understand what Wittgenstein was up to here, it is important to note that not only was he not a member of the Vienna Circle, he was not even a logical positivist. His work in the *Tractatus* was actually directed at resisting the scientization of all knowledge. The positivists held that what we can speak about meaningfully is all that really matters in human life. But Wittgenstein, as his friend Paul Engelman (1967) explained, passionately believed that what we must be silent about is actually all that really matters in human life. Ethics, aesthetics, metaphysics—these are what is truly important, even though we cannot make meaningful (scientific) statements about such matters. In the *Tractatus* Wittgenstein wrote: "It is impossible for there to be propositions of ethics," adding, propositions can express nothing that is "higher." That is, "Ethics is transcendental."

So, in spite of the interpretation of the logical positivists, Wittgenstein was not attempting to privilege science by showing that it alone contained meaningful statements, but rather simply pointing out that only scientific statements were capable of being verified. And in doing this, as Engelman noted, he was attempting to delimit the *unimportant* (the statements of science). "We feel that even when *all possible* scientific questions are answered, the problems of life remain completely untouched." (*Tractatus*, 6.52) As Engelman summed it up: "It is not the coastline of the island he is bent on surveying with such meticulous accuracy, but the boundary of the ocean (1967, p. 97).

For almost 10 years after completing the *Tractatus* Wittgenstein abandoned philosophy, returning to Austria to teach in elementary schools, and for a time even working as a gardener. When he returned to Cambridge in 1929 to teach, he began to reshape his philosophical outlook. In the *Tractatus*, Wittgenstein had attempted to demarcate scientific statements from other kinds of knowledge by the criterion of verification: Only scientific statements can be verified; hence, they alone are meaningful. He did not explain how scientific statements are verified; this, however, did become the project of the Vienna Circle, especially of Rudolph Carnap (1929). But all such attempts proved unsuccessful.

The problems the logical positivists confronted in trying to explain verification were the same empirical and logical problems that have dogged empiricism since the time of Berkeley and Hume. The empirical problem, first pointed out by George Berkeley (1685-1753), is that if the mind knows only ideas (or concepts or propositions), then the mind can never know that what it knows *does* represent objective reality. All it can ever know are ideas (or concepts or propositions) about objective reality, ideas whose correspondence with objective reality can never be verified.

The second problem of verification, the logical problem first pointed out by David Hume (1711-76), is the problem of induction. That is, it is not logically possible to infer a general or universal statement from a singular statement, nor from any number of singular statements. Thus, no matter how many black ravens one observes—"This is a black raven," "This is another black raven," and so on, one cannot validly infer (induce) the statement, "All ravens are black." Since most scientific statements are universal statements ("All planets revolve in an elliptical orbit," "All atoms have Nuclei," etc.), then it is logically impossible to verify these scientific statements by induction.

By the end of the 1920s, Wittgenstein came to recognize that scientific statements cannot be verified. If this is so, then the criterion of verification could not be used to demarcate scientific statements from other kinds of knowledge. It became imperative for him to devise another way of limiting the boundaries of science (or scientific statements) if other kinds of knowledge (like metaphysics, ethics, and aesthetics) were to be safeguarded.

During the next 20 years, Wittgenstein developed his "later philosophy," drawing around himself a coterie of disciples. He published nothing of this later philosophy during his lifetime, and it was not until 1953, two years after his death, that the later philosophy appeared in print under the title, *Philosophical Investigations*.

The later philosophy is a radical turnabout from the earlier *Tractatus*, where Wittgenstein had tried to preserve "high" knowledge from the inroads of science by limiting science to statements that can be verified. In *Philosophic Investigations*, he completely abandons the matter of verification and takes up instead the question of meaning. The meaning of a statement, he announces, is to be found in its use in a particular language game, or better, in its use by a specific linguistic community. There are many different language games or linguistic communities; hence, there are always many different meanings of any statement. There are no essential, or absolute, or true, meanings—meaning is always relative to a specific linguistic community. In consequence, Wittgenstein concludes, there are no philosophical problems, but only problems of language, problems that arise when people use language in odd ways, ways that violate the ordinary usage of a particular linguistic community, or the rules of a particular language game.

The important point about this linguistic turn in philosophy is that philosophers—at least Wittgenstein and his followers—now abandoned the search for truth and replaced it with a search for meaning.

This shift from a search for truth to a search for meaning was a consequence of Wittgenstein's quest for certainty. That is, for Wittgenstein, as for most philosophers since Plato, only that of which we are certain can be classified as knowledge. Having recognized that there is no way to justify a statement as true, Wittgenstein now saw that statements *can* be justified as meaningful: A statement is meaningful when it coheres with or corresponds to the ordinary or normal use of some linguistic community. He then suggests that a meaningful statement is one that is certain ("I know = I am familiar with it as a certainty," Wittgenstein wrote in *On Certainty* [1969], para. 271).

According to Wittgenstein, philosophers were not to legislate the meanings of statements but rather were simply to analyze how they were used by various language communities and then describe what they found. All so-called philosophical problems, therefore, were linguistic problems; such problems, then, were not to be solved, they were to be dissolved by uncovering the linguistic confusions.

THE INFLUENCE OF THE LATER PHILOSOPHY OF WITTGENSTEIN

A number of important consequences stem from the shift from the pursuit of truth to the pursuit of meaning. First, all knowledge now becomes relative. Meaning is relative to a language community. From this, it follows that all meaningful statements have equal footing. No longer are only scientific statements meaningful, as Wittgenstein had proposed in the *Tractatus*, and as the logical positivists had argued. Now, the statements made in *any* language game, by *any* linguistic community, are of equal worth—each has a meaning in that language game. This ushers ethics, aesthetics, and metaphysics back into the realm of meaningful discourse; but it also holds the door open for alchemy, astrology, voodooism—any language game practiced in any linguistic community.

Wittgenstein put it this way in *On Certainty*, published posthumously in 1969:

> Is it wrong for me to be guided in my actions by the propositions of physics? Am I to say I have no good ground for doing so? Isn't precisely this what we call a "good ground." (para. 608)

> Supposing we met people who did not regard that as a telling reason. Now, how do we imagine this? Instead of the physicist, they consult an oracle. (And for that we consider them primitive.) Is it wrong for them to consult an oracle and be guided by it?— If we call this "wrong" aren't we using our language game as a base from which to *combat* theirs? (para. 609)

> And are we right or wrong to combat it? Of course there are all sorts of slogans which will be used to support our proceedings. (para. 610)

> Where two principles really do meet which cannot be reconciled with one another, then each man declares the other a fool and a heretic. (para. 611)

> I said I would "combat" the other man,—but wouldn't I give him *reasons*? Certainly; but how far do they go? At the end of reasons comes *persuasion*. Think what happens when missionaries convert natives. (para. 612)

This new equality of all knowledge signals the end of criticism or critical discourse: Any and every statement is justified, that is, is acceptable, is certain, if it is part of some language game. And because there are no essential meanings, criticism between linguistic communities as to how the other community uses language is simply irrelevant and otiose. Description replaces argument and criticism: One describes what a statement means to a particular linguistic community and such understanding results in acceptance—that *is* the meaning of the statement for that group.

Of course, each of us must decide which meanings we will personally accept. Much of this is already decided for us by the mere fact that we each do grow up in particular linguistic communities and participate in their language games. But there are always many questions we must decide for ourselves. And because we cannot decide among different statements on the basis of truth, we must decide on the basis of our values, our commitments, our beliefs. This inevitably politicizes all questions. This happens because, as Nietzsche said, what people value is always that which serves their own well being, their own interests. Therefore, it follows that all disputed questions are disputes about the self-interests of the disputants—that is, politics.

In place of argument and critical discussion, disputants now use rhetoric and propaganda—appeals to the self-interests of listeners and readers. Indeed, from this angle of vision, all so-called arguments and critical discussions are actually masked rhetoric and propaganda. Critical analysis does not disappear, but now it functions to penetrate or "see through" arguments, claims, and presentations of all sorts in order to uncover the real intentions, the real self-interests, of those who present the arguments and claims.

Finally, this linguistic turn in philosophy creates a new world. By this I mean that the world is no longer given. Rather, because we humans create meaning, we create reality, create the world. We construe the world through language. We do not describe or represent what really is; we only create our knowledge, or make our meanings, and this is all the reality there is.

The later philosophy of Wittgenstein had a revolutionary impact on two generations of British and American philosophers, who carried out the research program charted by the master. In article after article and book after book, philosophers set out to describe the language games of the various disciplines. Books, monographs, and anthologies appeared with such titles as: The Language of Morals, The Logic of Historical Explanation, The Logic of the Social Sciences, The Logic of Religious Language, The Language of Education, The Language of Literary Criticism, The Language of Fiction.

Perhaps the most influential work that carried forward Wittgenstein's later philosophy was Thomas Kuhn's (1962/1970) *The Structure of Scientific Revolutions*. This book became the most frequently cited of all works in American scholarship for the next 25 years. Kuhn, a philosopher and historian of science, purported to describe how science really proceeds.

On his account, science at any given time is bounded by paradigms, a set of assumptions and beliefs within which research goes on. A paradigm is not derived from the observation of facts but rather is determinative of the facts that could possibly be observed. The reigning paradigms are guarded, licensed, and franchised by the existing elites—elites who train, indoctrinate, supervise, and socialize initiates into the scientific enterprise. The main activity for which initiates are trained is "normal science"—the solving of relatively minor problems, that is, "puzzles"—set by and in conformity with the reigning paradigm. Paradigms come and go. The adoption of a new paradigm is what Kuhn calls *revolutionary science*. But new paradigms emerge for no compelling reason other than an accumulation of doubts and vague dissatisfactions—anomalies—that challenge the earlier paradigm. The paradigms gain both ground and adherents simply because an older generation wedded to the defense of the older paradigm dies out. Once the new paradigm is established in the scientific community, it leads to the pursuit of "normal science," that is, all assume that the new paradigm is beyond question and beyond criticism, and all that remains is the solution of scientific "puzzles."

One paradigm, Kuhn insists, is as good as any other and is incommensurable with any other paradigm. Thus, one paradigm cannot be used to judge another. Scientists rewrite the textbooks not to chart progress toward the truth, but to suppress the resurgence of ideas already overthrown and to reinforce those in fashion or in power. Thus the history of science is the story of successive ideological hegemonies. In short, what drives science is not logic, but rhetoric; not critical argument, but persuasion. Indeed, Kuhn says that the force of scientific argument "is only that of persuasion." In the case of disagreements, "each party must try, by persuasion, to convert the other," and when one party succeeds, there is no higher court to which the outcome might be referred: "There is no standard higher than the assent of the relevant community." What better criterion, Kuhn asks, could there be? (1962/1970, 94-95, 170, 198)

In Kuhn's work we find all of the elements of the later philosophy of Wittgenstein made manifest. According to Kuhn, scientists have never searched for truth; they have always sought meaningful knowledge, knowledge that accorded with the paradigms accepted by their linguistic community. Nor do scientists discover reality; they construct it. And the knowledge they construct is relative to their community at a given time; modern science is not better than ancient science.[1] Moreover, according to Kuhn, scientists use persuasion, not critical arguments: "It is precisely the abandonment of critical discussion that marks the transition to science" (Kuhn, 1977, p. 273).

The later philosophy of Wittgenstein, with the help of scholars like Thomas Kuhn, created a new intellectual outlook that exerted a revolutionary impact on the humanities and the social sciences.

POST STRUCTURALISM IN LITERARY STUDIES

At an international symposium held at the Johns Hopkins Humanities Center in 1967 on the topic of structuralism, the French philosopher, Jacques Derrida, told the audience that structuralism was no longer an acceptable approach to literature. Structuralism assumed that the terms and statements used in a literary text have meaning within the structure of the text itself, but what established the meaning of the text itself? Derrida pointed out that the quest for the true meaning leads to an infinite regress. All words and texts, he explained, are indeterminate, giving rise to a multiplicity of meanings so numerous that they cancel each other out. Derrida concluded that there are no works of literature, only texts open to endless interpretation. The task of the literary critic, according to Derrida, is to deconstruct, that is, to uncover the inadequacy of any and all proposed interpretations of a text, thereby freeing readers from the burdens of imposed and illusory single meanings and making possible a variety of meanings suiting human needs (see Kernan, 1990, p. 81). In his speech at Johns Hopkins, Derrida explained that there are two interpretations of interpretation: One seeks to decipher truth; the other abandons truth and offers free play. Nietzsche, he said, showed us the second way, the way we should follow.

Derrida's speech made structuralism in literary scholarship passé. Humanist scholars, already unhappy with the threatened scientization of literature that structuralism seemed to promise, were only too happy to accept Derrida's logical arguments. They were

---

[1]Kuhn, in the expanded version of his book, tries to deny that he is a relativist and professes to believe in scientific progress (1962/1970, p. 206). Yet, he does reject the notion of truth, the notion that scientists are making better and better approximations of reality. The progress he refers to "is away from confusion, rather than toward any antecedent reality." But, at Bartley pointedly asks: "If one is less confused, what is one confused about? (1990, p. 29).

ready and anxious to take off in the direction he led, especially because the direction linked them to the later philosophy of Wittgenstein, which by now had a strong hold on the intellectual outlook of many academic fields. More than this, they recognized that this new intellectual outlook overcame the threat of marginalization of literary studies *without* increasing the risk of destroying literature itself.

Poststructuralist literary critics—like Jacques Derrida, Stanley Fish, and Frederick Jameson—leveled the same kind of criticism against structuralism that had been made against logical positivism: the impossibility of verification. These literary critics pointed out that the so-called hypothesis testing conducted by structuralists and stylisticians were logically invalid because they were either circular or led to an infinite regress. They are circular because the human mind knows only statements, which means that the structural properties those "scientists" claim to find in a work of literature are propositions (statements) that exist only in the minds of the scientists. We are, as Jameson (1972) put it, caught in the prison house of language. This predicament is also the source of the infinite regress these "scientists" fall into whenever they try to verify their claims about a text. For what a statement signifies or represents can only be—caught as we are in the prison house of language—another statement, which, of course, signifies or represents some other statement, which, or course, signifies or represents some other statement. And so it goes, into an infinite regress. This infinite regress makes verification impossible. Moreover, attempts to establish scientific models or structures of literary genre and literary periods run smack into the logical problems of induction: the logical impossibility of inferring a general statement about literature (or anything else) from any number of singular statements.

In abandoning the search for truth or for the true meaning of a text in order to pursue a multiplicity of meanings, not all poststructuralists are as accepting of the unlimited constructions of meanings of a text as is Derrida. Wolfgang Iser (1978), for example, sees the text itself as providing some limits or restrictions on what meanings can be constructed, whereas Stanley Fish (1973), in harmony with Wittgenstein, sees limits being imposed by the language community to which the reader belongs. Nevertheless, the poststructuralists are all in agreement that the task of the reader is to make meaning of the text, not to discover its meaning, and all agree that such meanings are subjective, hence relative to the reader.

This produces a multiplicity of meanings or interpretations of a text. By encouraging this multiplicity of meanings, poststructuralist literary scholars have created what Frederick Crews (1986) dubbed "the age of suspicion." That is, readers confronted with conflicting and incommensurable interpretations of a text, with no way of deciding which is correct, understandably shift their attention to the motives and intentions of the interpretators: What is he or she up to? From Nietzsche, the poststructuralists learned that every construction of knowledge, every interpretation, is one that serves the self-interest of the interpretator. From this, the poststructuralist concludes that the purpose of reading or writing is to control others. So, they approach all texts, or interpretations of texts, with questions such as: "What values or ideology is the interpreter trying to promote."

In this way all literature and all literary scholarship become politicized. Poststructuralists and their students attempt to "see through" the texts—both original literary texts, as well as texts purporting to interpret the original texts—in order to discover the conscious, or even unconscious, motivations of the authors.

A second generation of poststructuralist literary scholars has vigorously pursued this tack by uncovering the racism, sexism, imperialism, and elitism promoted by most of the literary works that make up the canon of western literature. This second generation points out that the established literary canon well served white, male, Protestant Europeans—enabling them to maintain cultural hegemony over blacks, women, and non-Anglo-Saxon ethnic groups.

The poststructuralists justify their own interpretations of literature as correct—politically correct—because they embody worthy and progressive values. Of course, a reader could come up with alternative interpretations of those same texts of western literature, but every interpretation must be assessed on its moral and/or political worthiness—there can be no other standard. Moreover, moral and political bases have also now become the grounds for choosing the texts for courses in literature: What matters is the social and political significance a text may have in raising the consciousness of students in combating the existing system of social control in our society.

Poststructuralists are a contentious lot, engaged in seemingly endless disputes with their adversaries and with one another. In these disputes, of course, they do not engage the critical arguments their opponents raise; instead, the poststructuralists try to penetrate the arguments of their opponents, to see through them, to uncover the motives of their opponents, to reveal whatever it is that their opponents are trying to impose on others.[2]

One of the most remarkable accomplishments of poststructuralism has been its dethroning of science as the paradigm for true

---

[2]For a classic example of this kind of uncovering, see Stanley Fish's (1989, pp. 202-211) treatment of the criticisms of William Jackson Bates.

knowledge. From the perspective of the poststructuralists, science consists solely of statements constructed by fallible human beings. Science, they conclude, is simply a genre of literature, an activity on the same footing as art, literature, and literary criticism—for, like the humanities, science is also a language game. Science, they insist, does not give us truth; rather, scientists simply construct meaning. Like literature and literary studies, science is subjective, relative, and not representational (of reality) simply because there is no foundation by which it can be justified. In the words of Richard Rorty, "Literature has now displaced religion, science and philosophy as the presiding discipline of our culture" (1982, p. 57).

3

Quantification in History and Anthropology

So far, I have argued that attempts in the 20th century to scientize the humanities wound up putting them at risk. The efforts of the logical positivists to scientize philosophy brought back with accelerated force the epistemological criticisms of empiricism first raised by Berkeley and Hume in the 18th century: criticisms that showed that it is logically and empirically impossible to verify statements about the real world. Later, the efforts of the new critics and structuralists to scientize literary studies likewise brought forth arguments that statements about literature cannot be verified. But if verification is not possible, then how is knowledge possible? How can philosophy or literary studies claim to be cognitive disciplines? To avert the risk of the disintegration of their disciplines, both philosophers and literary scholars abandoned their quest for truth and shifted to a quest for meaning. For both philosophers and literary scholars, statements were now justifiable not as true, but as meaningful, if they had meaning for some linguistic community. In the 1960s and 1970s some historians made this same epistemological shift, and here, too, this shift was precipitated by the computer.

MEANING AND HISTORY

By the end of the 1960s, many historians were employing computers to perform quantitative analyses, content analyses, and factor analyses of data. Especially in economic history, the use of the computer produced important new findings bearing on the economic conditions of the past. Yet, many professional historians remained suspicious. They remained suspicious because most traditional historians are humanists, and as humanists they cherish the idea of history as literature. They see the historian as an artist as well as a scholar: style, pace, and elegance are important—numbers break the rhythm of the prose. Carl Bridenbaugh (1984) shrilly warned historians never to "worship at the shrine of the bitch-goddess, QUANTIFICATION" (p. 326). In response to a survey conducted between 1967 and 1969 under the auspices of the Committee on Science and Public Policy of the National Academy of Sciences, and the Problems and Policy Committee of the Social Science Research Council—one historian declared that he did not think of himself as a social scientist because he considered it a "vile term."

Yet, the skepticism of the traditional historian was based on more than disagreement about esthetic priorities. As humanists, traditional historians know that many aspects of human conduct are not reducible to numbers. In another response to the 1967-69 survey, one historian said that as a humanist he believed "history is principally made of the ideas and actions of men, oftentimes unpredictable, and cannot be measured in statistical or 'scientific' terms" (Landes & Tilly, 1971, p. 31). The distinguished historian, Arthur M. Schlesinger, Jr., put it this way: "Almost all important questions are important precisely because they are not susceptible to quantitative analysis" (quoted in Landes & Tilly, 1971, p. 31).

Stephen Thernstrom, a Harvard historian, countered this sentiment in an influential article (1968). He argued that there are many historical problems of importance that demand the analysis of quantitative data—voting statistics, information on wages and prices, population figures, and so on. He went on to chastise historians for not taking advantage of "tons and tons" of untapped material in census material in census data, local tax returns, city directories, school attendance records, and so on.

During the 1960s, a number of computer-assisted quantitative studies appeared including Sidney Aronson's (1964) statistical critique of the myth of the Jacksonian spoils system, Lee Benson's (1961) reinterpretation of Jacksonian democracy, and Charles Tilly's (1975) study of the relationship between urbanization and counter-revolutionary political upheavals. In 1970, the first issue of the *Journal of Interdisciplinary History* marked the union between the quantitative social sciences and history, and in 1976 the Social Science History Association was created. By this time, the pages of traditional history journals had become more open to quantitative studies, and most of the major departments of history in the United States began to include one or more quantitative historians.

In becoming scientific, the quantitative historians did not, like their brethren in the natural sciences, look for general laws. Historians (most of them, anyway) recognize that history is "ideographic" not "nomethetic"; that is, history explains particular events, it does not seek to establish general laws. What quantitative historians did was to borrow the analytic methods of the social sciences to construct mathematical models and equations to simulate what happened in the past; they then measured and counted and used statistics to process their data.

The crux of the difference between traditional history and quantitative history is that traditional history tends to focus on specific individuals, or particular institutions, or particular ideas, and on nonrepetitive occurrences. In contrast to this, quantitative history focuses on collections of individuals, or categories of institutions, and repetitive occurrences. To explain this difference, one quantitative historian (Robert Fogel) supplied the following illustration:

> A traditional historian, for example, might want to explain why John Keats died at the time, in the way, and under the particular circumstances that he died. But to a social-scientific historian attempting to explain the course of mortality among the English, the particular circumstances of Keat's death might be less interesting than those circumstances that contribute to an understanding of why deaths due to tuberculosis were so frequent during the first half of the nineteenth century. (Fogel & Elton, 1983, p. 29)

To investigate the kinds of questions that concern them, quantitative historians not only lean heavily on quantitative evidence, but most actually produce such evidence through computer analyses of raw data that involve thousands and thousands of operations and, usually, the collaboration of many researchers.

Although quantitative history was first given systematic development in economic history, the utilization of the computer by other historians soon resulted in a "new social history," a history written "from the bottom up." That is, the computer now enabled historians to focus on groups—large groups—instead of individuals, about whom they gathered large aggregations of data concerning births, marriages, deaths, fortunes, occupations, schooling, religious status, and so on. By subjecting this data to sophisticated statistical analysis, historians produced in-depth historical accounts—"from the bottom up"—of migration, the family, industrialization, urbanization, and assimilation. One of the most outstanding studies of the early 1870s was Thernstrom's (1973) analysis of social mobility in Boston, which used the computer to draw together and analyze the life histories of thousands and thousands of men and women.

By the mid-1970s, some quantitative historians began to deride the efforts of traditional historians to reconstruct the motives and feeling of long dead individuals and allowed that however dramatic and compelling such attempts might be, they are beyond the reach of empirical inquiry and are better left to the evocative methods of poets. Traditional historians like Edward Kirkland, viewed such comments as threats to "retool, rethink, conform, or be plowed under" (Kirkland, 1967, p. 1494).

In 1974, Richard Fogel and Stanley Engelman published their highly controversial two-volume work, *Time on the Cross: The Economics of American Slavery*. With the publication of this work traditional historians had the opportunity to fight back. Although highly technical quantitative historical studies had appeared before, *Time on the Cross* was a historiographical landmark concerned with major issues that had broad implications for the interpretation of American history. Using mathematics and theoretically complex analyses together with intensive computer analyses of extensive banks of historical data, the authors put forth a number of remarkable contentions: the material condition of slaves was better than had been portrayed by other historians; the slave system did not produce economic stagnation and depression in the antebellum south; and it did not prevent economic growth in the region. The controversies sparked by the book clearly revealed that few historians had the training required to criticize the mathematical foundations and the statistical methods employed in the study.

Yet, criticize it they did. And critical discussion soon carried over into a searching reappraisal of the quantitative approach to history. The numerous journal articles and the especially convened symposia and conferences did uncover some of the inadequacies of computer-based historiography.

But in the critical discussion that ensued, traditional historians found quantitative historians turning back the same criticisms at traditional history. Once again, the problem of verification was at the core of the critical discussion: Can historians—quantitative or traditional—verify the statements they make about the past?

So, although the extended debates on quantitative history did uncover some of the weaknesses and pitfalls inherent in such an approach to an understanding of the past, the more important consequence was for the entire field of history itself. The critical environment generated by quantitative history had forced all historians to make explicit many of the assumptions that had hitherto remained implicit in historical investigation. Thus, when it became clear that the computer programs the quantitative historian employed actually stipulated what data they selected and what analyses they made of that data, it also brought forth the realization that this is no different from what traditional historians do: All historians approach the past with a mind set, a point of view that determines what they produce as history.

Here, the historians confronted the same empirical and logical obstacles that faced the literary critics: There is no way to verify what historians say about the past, just as there is no way to verify what literary critics say about a text. So, in history as in literary studies, the computer had created a crisis. If history was not objective, if historians did not and could not tell us the truth about the past, then what was history for? What were historians up to?

In the field of history, as in the case of literary studies, practitioners now tried to avert risk by turning from the pursuit of truth to a quest for meaning. In 1970, Howard Zinn published the highly influential *The Politics of History*. According to Zinn,

> The historian is thus free to give one meaning or another to past events. I can choose, by the way I tell the story, to make World War I seem a glorious battle between good and evil, or I can make it seem a meaningless massacre. There is no inherently true story of World War I if some absolute, objective past is sought— there is only the question of which version is true to which present purpose. There is only the meaning created by the historian—a meaning represented by the effect on those who listen to the story. (p. 275)

Zinn went on to say that the meaning of what a historian writes is found not in his intention, nor in what he literally says, but "in the effect of his writing on human beings. An idea fulfills its meaning at the moment when, by its effect on others it becomes an act. By writing history, we engage in an act which (through the reader) has consequences, large or small, on behalf of human values or in opposition to them" (p. 280).

History, from this point of view, inexorably becomes politicized. Zinn rejects "disinterested scholarship" and "objectivity" as myths. The only criterion for acceptable history he permits is not that it advances the understanding of the past, but that it advances politically correct values.

The following year, the first edition of the two-volume textbook entitled *The Underside of American History* (Frazier, 1971) was published. It was a collection of readings that dealt with a variety of oppressed groups in America: Indians, indentured servants, blacks, Irish and German Catholics, women, and children. The intent of this project, according to the editor, was to point out that many of the problems of America today have their roots in the past and suggest that without resolution of the social and economic inequities of American life, conflict, stress, and repression will continue to characterize much of American society. Here, then was history presented in order to promote politically correct values.

In no time at all, historians' concern with victimization boiled over into accusations that all past historiography has fostered oppression and victimization by presenting history from the point of view of white, male, Europeans. This spawned new accounts of the past, accounts that forthrightly presented history from the point of view of the victims: feminist history, Indian (later Native American) history, Black (later, African-American) history. These new accounts of the past not only took a new point of view, they also attempted to "see through" the earlier histories by revealing the rhetoric and ideology earlier historians had used to support and further oppression and victimization.

By the mid-1970s, many historians had abandoned the traditional goal of detachment and now openly admitted, even professed, their emotional or ideological commitments. In the introduction to *The Enlightenment in America* (1976), Henry May wrote: "One thing that has been forced on university teachers by their students in recent years is that they abandon the comforting pose of academic impartiality and declare their allegiances, even—contrary to all their training—admit their emotions" (p. xvii). In his 1975 presidential address to the American Historical Association, Gordon Wright, while not himself abandoning the search for truth, told his fellow historians: "Our search for truth ought to be quite consciously suffused by a commitment to some deeply held human values" (1976, p. 2).

In a volume on contemporary historical writing that he edited for the American Historical Association called *The Past Before Us*, Michael Kammen (1980) noted the self-critical turn in historical writing:

> Liberalism and the liberal tradition in the United States have been challenged. The motives of national leaders are discussed cynically; and the makers of American foreign policy have been fiercely chastised on the basis of revisionist historical research. Unqualified affirmations of the national past now seem simplistic and embarrassing. (p. 22)

This turn toward a quest for meaning in history provoked criticism from some historians. In an assessment of the new social history, Theodore Rabb (1982) noted how the concern for meaning has unleashed much incoherence in the field. He admitted that this kind of history has multiplied the pluralism of current historical research to include such events as the examination of some of the inhabitants of a historical village in France, an eccentric miller in Italy, the diary of a clergy in England, or descriptions of a ritual in Bali. However, he went on to point out that the painstaking and exhaustive atomizing of a confined body of data undermined, and perhaps made impossible, the construction of larger patterns of the past. And without a larger vision, Rabb claimed, the details lose their significance (pp. 318-321).

Yet, the logic of the situation created by the turn toward meaning in history has done more than generate a multiplicity of arcane research projects. It has also provided a number of incommensurable interpretations of the same event. Rabb reminded readers how fundamentally the interpretations of the inner life of early modern Frenchmen given in *The Peasants of Languedoc* (Ladurie, 1979) by LeRoy Ladurie conflicts with the interpretations of Natalie Z. Davis in "The Reasons of Misrule," in *Society and Culture in Early Modern France* (Davis, 1975). This proliferation of conflicting meanings, with no way of deciding among them, creates uncertainty in the minds of readers and makes them suspicious of the motives of historians. (Many historians, of course, would say that readers *should* be suspicious.)

For some traditional historians, this turn from a search for truth about the past to a search for the meaning of the past has leveled a devastating blow to history itself. They accuse revisionist historians of imposing on the past whatever meanings accord with their own world view or ideology. "Now," Oscar Handlin, one of these traditional historians, lamented, "truth and untruth become matters of choice and fact yielded to intuition" (1979, p. 157). Another, Gertrude Himmelfarb, has lamented "abandoning not only the conventions regarding the presentation and documentation of evidence, but the very idea of objective evidence, reasoning, coherence, consistency, factuality" (1994, p. 158).

History now joined the other humanities—philosophy and literary studies—in affirming that there is no objective truth: The professional concern of historians is with meaning, which is subjective and relative—something that historians construct, not discover. Moreover, the choice among meanings is a value judgment, which means that historians should choose those meanings that promote human and progressive values. History, like philosophy and literary studies, has been politicized.

POSTMODERN ANTHROPOLOGY

The last of the humanities (or human sciences) I discuss is anthropology—the study of human beings. Most anthropologists have assumed the unity of humanity and have attempted to explain that unity in the face of the many diverse cultures human beings have created. The 19th-century anthropologists couched their explanations in the language of evolution. That is, according to early anthropologists like Edward Taylor (1832-1917), human beings evolved from a primitive state to a civilized one, which meant that cultures could be situated in an evolutionary continuum. A second theory was that of diffusion, promoted by George Boas (1858-1942). Here, the contention was that innovations in one culture were transmitted or "diffused" to other cultures. There is a logical similarity between these theories insofar as one (evolutionary anthropology) holds that cultures emerge slowly over time, whereas the other (diffusion) holds that cultures expand slowly over space.

But whether spatial or temporal, the bother with such theories is that they deny the equality of human beings. Primitive cultures, primitive people, were construed as inferior: They were uncivilized and had primitive minds. At least this was the criticism leveled by Bronislaw Malinkowski (1884-1942), the Polish-born, English anthropologist, who was the creator of the functionalist theory. According to functionalism, every culture has its own internal dynamics that the anthropologist must uncover. So-called primitive cultures are not early, inferior versions of civilized culture, the functionalists maintain. As the functionalists see it, each culture has its own arrangements—beliefs, values, understandings, attitudes, institutions, rituals—that "fit" that culture and perform a necessary function within it. What are universal to all human beings are the arrangements that exist in every culture, for example, marriage, religion, property. These arrangements take different forms in order to fit into a given culture, but essentially they are similar insofar as they perform functions necessary for the survival of the culture. In order to obtain a truly scientific understanding of the arrangements of other cultures, Malinowski insisted that anthropologists engage in intensive and long-term field study (empirical observation) of the daily lives of native peoples.

After World War II, a new anthropological theory emerged: structuralism. In contrast to functionalism, which regarded cultural phenomena as utilitarian, structuralists like Claude Levi-Strauss (1908-) claim that cultural phenomena are the result of the cognitive structures all human beings share. Structuralism first emerged, as we saw earlier, in the field of linguistics, when Ferdinand Saussure (1857-1913) claimed to have traced language to the innate structures of the mind. If the mind *is* regulated by structures or universal laws, then, Levi-Strauss (1963) argued, these structures will determine or inform all human behavior and all forms of social life. Thus, both language and culture are the products of the unconscious mind. Structural anthropology, like the science of linguistics, aims at discovering general laws. But, unlike functional anthropology, structuralists move beyond the empirical observation of institutions and behavior into the cognitive realm, where they seek to discover the cognitive structures or principles that underlie behaviors and institutions. These, Levi-Strauss maintains, are fundamentally mathematical.

Thus, structuralism calls for the progressive mathematization of anthropology, a project reminiscent of Leibnitz's universal mathematics. Levi-Strauss has used algebra to interpret marriage laws, as well as to analyze variants of myths. He has also used scalograms in the structural study of hierarchical variants in social organizations.

In the 1960s and the 1970s, the field became more and more mathematized as anthropologists increasingly used the computer for the processural analysis of social cultural systems.[1] The computer also enabled researchers to devise mathematical models of residence, marriage alignment, recruitment to social groups, and acceptance of innovation that could be compared to actual ethnographic data. Another area of mathematization was the optimizational analysis of behavior. Here researchers employed the new mathematical methods of game theory, decision theory, and linear programming to study political problems (e.g., the problems of succession and secession), economic problems (e.g., the effects of the introduction into a culture of a new commodity, a new crop, a new technology), and social problems (e.g., the number of wives people acquire).

---

[1] In what follows I have relied heavily on Douglas White (1973).

Anthropologists during this period also began to use mathematics to determine the social, cultural, and cognitive structures that underlie marriage patterns and kinship relations. Here they used graph theory and matrix analysis to reduce complex bodies of ethnographic data to a finished model that displays the structural properties sought.

Anthropologists also began to use mathematics for what they call *decomposition*—the reduction of complex systems to the elements and operational rules that govern the combinations of elements. Here finite mathematics and abstract algebra helped to identify the rules that govern such cultural phenomena as address terms, kinship terminology, group marriage rules, and social networks.

The sharpened and intensified scientization of anthropology made possible by computers triggered the same epistemological and moral criticisms that rocked the fields of literature and history. Here, too, critics of scientization rolled out the ancient criticisms against empiricism and induction, along with the long-standing moral criticisms humanists have made against science.

The empirical criticism, once again, was that it is not possible to confirm or verify claims that anthropologists make about peoples and cultures. It is not possible to compare such claims with ethnographic data because anthropologists, like the rest of us, are trapped in the prison house of language (or the prison house of conceptions, theories, ideas, or whatever it is that the mind knows). Actually, most of these critics of traditional, or so-called modern anthropology, use the term *text*: A culture is a text, and what people say and write about a culture is also a text. So, we are trapped in the prison house of texts: We cannot confirm, or verify, or justify a claim about culture because both the culture and the claims about it are texts; therefore, we cannot transcend texts in order to confront empirical reality.

In addition to rejecting the empirical foundation of modern anthropology, critics also pointed out the logical invalidity of generalizations—the so-called laws, universal principles, or universal characteristics of human beings—that modern anthropologists had inferred (induced) from the mountains of particular facts (ethnographic data) they obtained from field observation. Induction is logically impossible.

These criticisms gave birth to what is called postmodern anthropology, the most salient characteristic of which is the notion that what anthropologists tell us about other people and other cultures are not objective truths but simply subjective interpretations. Furthermore, all the arguments anthropologists provide to substantiate the interpretations they present are not logical arguments to prove that their interpretations are true, but merely rhetorical arguments to persuade readers to accept these interpretations.

As these postmoderns reject the true and objective representation of culture because it is empirically and logically impossible,
and because they allow only the interpretation of culture, then, once
again, the only basis for deciding among competing interpretations is
morality or politics.

In the past, according to the postmodernists, most modern
anthropologists, whether by design or not, provided interpretations of
other cultures that accorded with or buttressed western imperialism.
Thus, modern anthropologists studied safe topics such as marriage,
kinship, family, or the technologies of basket weaving, instead of analyzing the larger political and economic system that was responsible
for the unhappy circumstances of the people they studied. Some postmoderns have made an even more sweeping moral condemnation of
"anthropological science," maintaining that construing anthropology
as a science is dehumanizing, insofar as the anthropologist then
treats his or her subjects not as human agents, but as objects to be
observed and analyzed. Anthropology, they argue, if it is to become a
truly *human* science, must begin to treat all people as equally
human, as agents.

One of the leading lights of postmodern anthropology is
Clifford Geertz, whose highly influential work, *The Interpretation of
Cultures* (1973), has served as a kind of manifesto for the interpreta-
tive turn in anthropology. Geertz forthrightly declares that anthropology is "not an experimental science in search of law, but an interpretive one in search of meaning" (p. 9). Sometimes called the
Wittgenstein of anthropology, Geertz has acknowledged that his mis-
sion has been to inform anthropologists about the revolutionary
thoughts of the later Wittgenstein. Thus, he points out that "cultures
consist of socially established structures of meaning" in terms of
which people conduct their lives. The anthropologist's task is to interpret culture, to construct meanings of other people's constructions of
what they and their compatriots are up to. What the anthropologist
presents is "not scientifically tested and approved hypotheses" but
rather "fictions" in the sense that they are "something made" or
"something fashioned." Instead of "describing" or "explaining," the
anthropologist "inscribes" and "specifies" (p. 15). That is, through
"thick description" of social actions, he or she inscribes the meaning
that particular actions have for the actor, from whom those actions
originate, and then, he or she specifies by stating what the knowledge thus obtained demonstrates about the society in which it is
found and about social life as such (p. 27).

Not for Geertz the discovery of the essence of human nature,
nor the uncovering of the laws of culture. No, for him the purpose is
simply "to bring us into touch with the lives of strangers." In his own

work, Geertz has analyzed such matters as violence, identity, legiti-
macy, revolution, status, and death, interpreting "particular
attempts by particular people to place these things in some sort of
comprehensible, meaningful frame" (p. 30). The essential vocation of
interpretive anthropology "is not to answer our deepest questions,
but to make available to us answers that others, guarding other
sheep in other valleys, have given, and then to include them in the
consultable record of what man has said" (p. 30).

There is, of course, no way to confirm or verify the interpretations that anthropologists provide of other cultures, so why should
anyone accept any anthropologist's interpretation of a given culture?
The answer, of course, is that nonanthropologists should accept
whatever interpretation is accepted by the community of anthropologists. This community of experts should be taken as an epistemic
authority. Of course, there will always be subgroups within the community of anthropologists, subgroups who play different language
games, or subgroups who accept one interpretation and reject the
interpretations accepted by other subgroups. Like the new social history and poststructural literary studies, there is pluralism in postmodern anthropology. Each interpretation is said to be of equal intellectual worth. In this relativist intellectual world, there is no way to
ascertain which interpretation is true. One can choose among different and competing interpretations only on moral or political grounds.

Some postmoderns expand these moral concerns so far as to
make them skeptical about whatever any anthropologist writes about
another culture. Stephen Tyler, for example, rejects the ideology of
observer-observed: "There being nothing observed and no one who is
an observer" (1986, p. 126). Tyler opts for "the dialogical production
of a discourse, a story of sorts." This cooperative story telling, he
says, "would have the final word in framing the story (p. 126).
Meaning is not in the story presented, even if the story is dialogically
produced. Rather, the story *evokes* meaning in the reader. The whole
point of "evoking", Tyler explains, is that it frees ethnography from
representation and "the inappropriate mode of scientific rhetoric"
that entails 'objects', 'facts', 'descriptions', 'induction', 'generalizations', 'verification', 'experiment', 'truth', and like concepts that,
except as empty invocations, have no parallels either in the experience of ethnographic fieldwork, nor in the writing of ethnographies"
(pp. 129-130).

Tyler also raises strong moral criticisms against traditional
anthropology because—although representation is impossible—some
modern anthropologists continue to claim that what they present is a
true representation of other cultures. They are simply trying to control, Tyler warns. And even a postmodern anthropologist who presents

his or her own interpretation of another culture is likewise attempting to control. To attempt to control is immoral, and the guarantee against such attempts is to welcome and embrace a plurality of interpretations of cultures. From this, Tyler concludes that it is morally correct to reject the scientific prejudice about clear, unambiguous, objective, and logical expression because the meanings an ethnographic text evoke are paradoxical and enigmatic. As Tyler sees it, what the interpretive anthropologist is dealing with—meaning—is "not so much ineffable as over-effable, possessing a surplus of effability, so that the infinite possibility of its effability becomes the condition of its ineffability, and the interpretation of a text must struggle against the surplus of meaning, not with its obscurity or poverty" (p. 136).

Like literature, history, and the other humanities, anthropology, in its efforts to avert the risk of scientization made possible by the coming of the computer, has abandoned the quest for truth and taken up instead the search for meaning.

4

THE RISK-FREE
INTELLECTUAL WORLD

In Part One I argued that the coming of the electronic computer has led scholars in the humanities and the social sciences to create a risk-free intellectual world. The advent of the computer heralded the scientization of all realms of knowledge. Armed with the computer, scholars saw the possibility of mathematizing literary studies, history, and anthropology. They believed that once they were mathematized, the humanities would become *human* sciences, able to stand beside the physical and biological sciences as legitimate fields of knowledge.

But to many other humanist scholars, the promise of mathematization constituted a threat to the humanities. For unlike physical scientists, who study activities like the motions of the planets or the growth of plants, the goings-on that concern literary scholars, historians, and anthropologists are human goings-on—human conduct. Whereas in the physical world all goings-on are determined, or take place in accord with physical laws, human goings-on are thought to be the outcome of intelligence or human choice. In consequence, these critical humanist scholars perceived the scientization of their fields as the acceptance of determinism in human conduct and the denial of human agency. This in their eyes was tantamount to destroying the essence of the humanities.

To counteract this threat of the disintegration of their fields, a number of these resistant humanist scholars launched an all-out attack on the epistemological and moral foundations of the scientific approach. In literary scholarship, this movement was usually called poststructuralism; in history it was sometimes called the new social history; and in anthropology, it came to be called postmodernism. In what follows, I use the term *postmodernism* to refer to this movement in all of the humanities.

In their attack against scientization, the postmodernists revived and took seriously the criticisms of empiricism and induction that Berkeley and Hume had made in the 18th century. Applying these criticisms to their own fields, they demonstrated that statements about the real world—about the past, about literature, about other cultures—cannot be confirmed or logically validated. There is no way to justify any such statement as true. For, according to this argument, we are all caught in the prison of language, or, put another way, there is no way to prove that what is in the mind of the scholar—mental events—does in fact represent what is going on in the real world -- material events. Moreover, we cannot infer (induce) any true generalization about the past, about literature, or about other cultures, because induction—drawing universal statements from a number of particular statements—is logically invalid.

With these arguments, these critics sought to abolish the "common-sense" epistemology of the modern world—that epistemology which holds that we receive our knowledge through the careful observation of the real world. In its place, postmodern humanist scholars installed a new epistemology: the epistemological constructionism of Nietzsche and his continental followers. According to constructionism, human beings do not receive knowledge, they construct it, they make it up. These postmodern humanists then partnered the constructionism of Nietzsche with the justificationism of Wittgenstein, who had pointed out that although statements about the world cannot be justified as true, they can be justified as meaningful. According to Wittgenstein, a statement is justified as meaningful when it is commonly accepted or used by some linguistic community in some language game. By construing their own endeavors in the humanities as a quest for meaning, not truth, the postmodern scholars cast themselves as interpreters, not explainers. They take as their scholarly task the interpretation of the meaning of the past, or of a literary text, or of a culture. Interpretations, of course, are subjective, not objective—all the more so because they are constructed, not discovered. So there is no foundation, no essence, on which to base our knowledge of a text, our knowledge of the past, or our knowledge of other cultures. Postmoderns conclude that our knowledge does not represent what is really "out there."

Although most humanist scholars tend to their own gardens, it is not lost on them, and some of their number even point out, that the epistemological criticisms that have turned their own fields upside down apply equally to the physical and the biological sciences. Scientists in these fields, the postmodernists say—and here they cite Thomas Kuhn—do not give us objective knowledge either. They do not give us true explanations of the goings-on in the world. Rather, physical scientists are interpreting and attempting to impose their interpretations on us. These interpretations or meanings are simply those shared by a particular linguistic community at a particular time and place, and the existence of that community constitutes the sole epistemic authority for so-called science. (Paul Gross and Norman Levitt [1994, p. 8] maintain that the postmodernist attacks on science are not based on fact and logic but are simply acts of moral one-upmanship.)

The upshot of the postmodern revolution in the humanities is the emergence of a risk-free intellectual world: a world where logical criticism does not exist. For, if justified knowledge is not true knowledge, but simply any statement that has meaning to some linguistic community, then *whatever* one says, writes, or publishes about the goings-on in the world is immunized from criticism so long as one can point to some linguistic community that subscribes to the statement. In the traditional intellectual world, whatever one said, wrote, or published, was open to criticism and to demands for proof that it was true. But in the subjective, relativistic, world of postmodernism, criticism and demands for proof have no place. Professors, and students too, can write and speak about goings-on with impunity. Understandably, professors and students welcome the intellectual freedom provided to them in this risk-free intellectual world—the freedom from intellectual criticism of whatever they say or write.

However, in this risk-free intellectual world of postmodernism, moral or political criticism *is* possible and *is* encouraged. That is, even though a statement or theory may be justified because it is accepted by some linguistic community, no linguistic community is cognitively superior to any other; all are on an even footing. From this it follows that no one should be allowed to make statements that harm or adversely affect people who belong to some other group or community. So, although there is no way to ascertain what statements about the past, about other cultures, or about literature are true—because all such statements are actually interpretations—we can, nevertheless, decide which interpretations to reject on moral and political grounds: We should criticize and reject those interpretations that are morally wrong or politically incorrect—those statements that harm or adversely affect others.

This introduction of moral considerations has led to a searching reappraisal of traditional modern scholarship in the humanities and has resulted in a wholesale trashing of much of it. Traditional humanist scholarship, postmodernists assert, is tainted with racism, sexism, elitism, and imperialism. These moral evils, the postmoderns say, came about not by design but rather are the inevitable outcome of the fact that humans construct their knowledge. For, as Nietzsche pointed out, when human beings construct knowledge, what they construct is always what will serve their own self-interests. Hence, as almost all earlier humanist scholars were white males of European descent, the argument continues, the knowledge that they constructed about the past, about literary texts, and about other cultures, served *their* interests and not the interests of blacks, women or non-Western people. In consequence, the postmodernists point out, the traditional scholarly work in the humanities—in literature, in history, in anthropology—has been inherently racist, sexist, and imperialist.

The only possible defense against the acts of oppression committed by traditional humanist scholars is to construe all interpretations as being equal. Thus, postmodern thought generated a strong commitment to the ideology of egalitarianism. All interpretations of literary works—of the past, of other cultures—were to be viewed as equal; none were to be privileged.

More than this: the acts of oppression committed by traditional humanist scholars were simply manifestations of what was inherent in the culture itself. So from the point of view of postmodern thought, the traditional culture is the source of oppression. Constructed as it was by the most powerful and influential groups, that culture—the social, political, and economic arrangements— served their interests at the expense of the rest of the people. Thus, the traditional culture places many of us at risk. And, once again, the only possible defense against an oppressive culture is to create more equal cultural arrangements. The present culture must be transformed so that no group is privileged and none has hegemony. Only an egalitarian culture can eliminate the risk of oppression.

It is this postmodern intellectual outlook—an outlook that developed in the wake of the electronic computer—that launched risk aversion throughout society. For most, but not all, humanist scholars have taken up this postmodern intellectual outlook and have promulgated it in books, articles, and in their teaching. As a result, many, but not all, liberal arts graduates over the last 25 years have learned to subscribe to the notion that all knowledge is subjective and relative: No statement can be justified as true, it can only be justified as certain (i.e., meaningful) if it is accepted by a particular linguistic community. They have also learned that statements can only be judged on moral and political grounds and criticized and rejected insofar as they harm members of other groups. And, finally, they have learned to be suspicious of the traditional culture—the "system"—because most of the statements that do harm people are emanations of that traditional culture.

In the remainder of the book I try to show how this intellectual outlook of postmodernism precipitated a risk-aversive response to the mathematization of culture that the computer made possible.

PART TWO

A RISK-AVERSIVE POLITY

5

HEALTH, SAFETY, AND ENVIRONMENTAL RISKS

In 1980, a Louis Harris poll found that four-fifths of those surveyed agreed that "people are more subject to risk today than they were twenty years ago." Only 6% thought there was less risk.

On the face of it, these fears seem overblown and irrational because experts tell us that the level of danger in society has not gone up in recent years—indeed, there seems to be less risk: Life expectancy is longer than ever before; polio, smallpox, and other infectious diseases have been all but eradicated; we now have the know-how to construct buildings much better able to withstand powerful earthquakes; and improved weather observation and reporting warn people of approaching hurricanes. Moreover, harm to health caused by accidents or food was far more prevalent in the past; in point of fact, people at the same age are healthier than they once were, except for the very old because so few made it that far in the past.

Yet, there is abundant evidence that more and more Americans are anxious—anxious about the future, anxious about their safety, anxious about their health, anxious about their well-being. In 1981, a group of scholars from the Survey Research Center published a study comparing the life experiences of Americans in 1976 and 1957 (Veroff, Douvan, & Kulka, 1981). They found an increased concern about an uncertain future. In 1976, young people, especially, reported increased symptoms of anxiety and worry. By way of explanation, the authors pointed out that the job market for young people was unclear, family roles—both marriage and parenthood—were in transition, and commitments to family and work were harder for young people to make than they once were. (I note, in passing, that the young people's knowledge of the reality of their situation was based on statistical trends compiled by the computers of economists and other social scientists.)

One need not rely on polls or surveys to see that America has become a risk-aversive society. The daily newspapers readily confirm this. I have before me a copy of the *New York Times* of August 13, 1992. On the front page there are two stories about risk aversion. One reports that the Federal Drug Administration (FDA) has too few staff members to keep up with the safety assessment of new products being introduced by drug companies. The second story is about the closing of a nuclear power plant in Ranier, Oregon—"a sign of nuclear power's decline," the *Times* reports.

On the editorial page there is a letter from Henry Heimlich (the inventor of the Heimlich maneuver to save choking victims), maintaining that the present administration of the Center for Disease Control has lost control. Dr. Heimlich points out the "syphilis rate is the highest in 40 years. There were 50,000 new cases in 1990. Tuberculosis exceeds a million cases. Last year measles infected 500 people in Philadelphia alone, killing 6 children—the first measles deaths in 20 years. Malaria, introduced by migrant workers, is increasing rapidly." In the "Science Times" section of the same edition of the newspaper, there is an article reporting that scientists have learned that low cholesterol may be just as dangerous to one's health as high cholesterol. The same page also contains a report about a new questionnaire that married couples can use to predict (94 times out of 100) whether they will still be married five years later. (The article starts out by reminding readers that 1 in 2 marriages ends in divorce.)

In May 1994 the U.S. Public Interest Research Group and the Consumer Federation of America issued a joint report announcing that 9 out of 10 children's playgrounds contain hidden hazards that are partly to blame for accidents that send some 170,000 youngsters to hospital emergency rooms every year.

Not too long ago I received a mail order catalogue from a company called "The Safety Zone" (the holiday edition, as it happens). This 64-page catalogue advertises safety products for the home, for the car, for children, for pets, for winter safety, and for travel, as well as for personal protection and home security. It includes gadgets for detecting lead in the home and other gadgets and kits for uncovering radon, natural gas, electromagnetic fields, and carbon monoxide.

WHY HAVE WE BECOME A RISK-AVERSIVE SOCIETY?

Have we become a nation of wimps? The late political scientist Aaron Wildavsky thought so. "How extraordinary," he exclaimed. "The richest, longest-lived, best-protected, most resourceful civilization, with the highest degree of insight into its own technology, is on its way to becoming the most frightened (1990, p. 120)." As Wildavsky saw it, there are not more risks today, there simply are more risk perceivers.

But why are there more risk perceivers?

For openers, there has been a significant shift in the nature of the health and environmental risks we encounter. We suffer and die not so much from infectious diseases like pneumonia, influenza, and tuberculosis, but from chronic degenerative diseases like cancer and heart diseases; and, although fewer are killed by national disasters or industrial accidents, more are killed in automobile crashes. Moreover, there has been an increase in new risks that are fundamentally different in both character and magnitude from those encountered in the past: nuclear war, nuclear power plant accidents, radioactive waste, exposure to synthetic pesticides, supertanker oil spills, chemical plant and storage accidents, recombinant DNA laboratory accidents, ozone depletion, and acid rain. Perhaps most important in explaining why there are more risk perceivers today is that these new, technologically induced risks have been the object of serious, intensive, scientific analysis over the last 20 years.

THE PROFESSIONALIZATION OF RISK ANALYSIS

Human beings are naturally risk aversive (otherwise, the species would not have survived), and we have always engaged in risk analysis.

As early as 3200 B.C. there lived in the Tigris-Euphrates Valley a group of priest-like oracles, called the Ashipo, who specialized in risk analysis. People consulted them regarding any forthcoming risky adventure—a journey, a marriage, a battle, a building site. For data, the Ashipo used signs from the gods. They would issue a report etched on a clay tablet in the form of a ledger, listing the favorable signs (a plus for each) along with the unfavorable ones (a minus for each). Risk analysis did not get much more sophisticated until Pascal invented probability theory in the 17th century. In time, probability theory came to be used to calculate risk in the fields of insurance, epidemiology, and gambling.

In the last half of the 20th century risk analysis became professionalized as scientists began to use the computer to calculate and measure the probable risks to human health and safety and to the environment.

THE QUANTIFICATION OF HEALTH RISKS

During the 20th century we have witnessed the increased quantification of human beings. Before this century, people did use numbers to provide a limited description of a person: He is 48 years of age, weighs 175 pounds, and is 5 feet 10 inches tall. Yet the use of age to categorize people was considerably less important up until this century: People did not always know how old they were. Not only was the notion of age blurred, but people also had only a rough idea of how much they weighed and how tall they were (Chudacoff, 1989). Before mid-century, few people owned their own bathroom scales—they got weighed at the doctor's office or weighed themselves for a penny on the scales at the drug store. Today, people not only know their precise age and exact weight and height, they also know their latest blood pressure reading, cholesterol level, and perhaps even their blood sugar count. Moreover, most people can tell you their average daily caloric intake.

The dream of quantification of the human body and all its functions has been around for a long time. Herophilus, an Alexandrian physician born in the last third of the 4th century B.C., was apparently the first person to count the pulse using a water clock. Yet, until the end of the 19th century, most physicians believed that sensorial judgments could not be improved by their quantification and thus ignored such measurements. But by the 20th century, physicians were not only counting the pulse, they were also using the newly invented thermometer to quantify body temperature. By this time, too, physicians had a reliable instrument for measuring and quantifying blood pressure and a machine that tracked the path of the heart's electrical current. This conversion of physiological signals into numbers and graphs made these physical processes objective and their meanings unambiguous and evident to all physicians. Now clear and accurate quantitative records could be kept for each patient so that changes in patterns could be studied over time.

Chemistry was used in the service of medical diagnosis as early as the 16th century when physicians focused on the visible features of urine to gain knowledge of a patient's illness. But it was not until the middle of the 19th century that there were any attempts at quantification. Beginning first with studies of the quantifiable relationship of sugar in the blood to diabetes and of uric acid in the blood to gout, physicians moved on to count red cells and the hemoglobin content of the blood. With the development of techniques of chemical analysis that used only small quantities of blood—as small as that obtained by a prick of the finger—most of the commonly tested components of blood serum could be quantitatively estimated: nonprotein nitrogen, urea, uric acid, creatinine, creatine, and sugar (Reiser, 1978).

By the mid-twentieth century, physicians were able to establish norms, averages, and ranges so that patients could see how well they and their bodily processes "measured up." But with the coming of the computer, each person's book of life began to be written exclusively in the language of mathematics—numbers, graphs, figures, tables—logged in obstetric records, medical examination records, hospital records, and death records that now charted one's passage from (pre) birth to the grave.

Not only has each of our lives become quantified, but, in addition, physicians (or their computers) can use this quantified data to perform factor analyses, discriminate analyses, and multivariate analyses that enable them to provide us with probabilistic diagnoses of our ailments and probabilistic prognoses of their cure. Computers are used for hypothesis testing and for performing measurements, that were never possible before, such as CAT scans and ultrasound antenatal diagnoses. Epidemiologists use computers to make more accurate estimations and predictions about the incidence and the spread of disease.

Today, most people are aware of the mortality rates in the United States, know what Americans die of, and recognize which geographic areas have the highest death rates. We have some notion of the probabilities of having a heart attack or a stroke; we know that high blood pressure causes strokes, and clogged arteries cause heart attacks. Moreover, we know that some foods cause clogged arteries, and other foods can cause high blood pressure. In recent years, as the Surgeon General reported in 1988, most of us have changed our diets to reduce the intake of foods that put our health at risk (Surgeon General's Report on Nutrition and Health, 1989).

Because of our fear of cholesterol, we now eat less meat and more fish and poultry, we eat and drink more low-fat milk products rather than those containing whole milk. We eat more vegetables and have substituted vegetable oils for animal oils. We have also cut down on our sugar consumption. And because of our fear that caffeine causes cancer, we have cut down on our consumption of coffee, and many of us have switched to decaffeinated coffee (although some recent studies tell us that decaffeinated coffee may be bad for our hearts). Recent news that margarine, popcorn, and hot dogs are bad for us, has further changed American diets, as have the reports that meat is harmful if it is fatty, chicken may carry salmonella, and fish may not have been properly inspected.

The modern concept of nutrition—that human life depends on a steady intake of a variety of specific dietary substances in defined amounts—is less than 200 years old. It began late in the 18th century when cod liver oil was first used as a treatment for rickets. At about the same time the British Navy introduced lemon juice to prevent scurvy. During the 19th century, knowledge of nutritional science grew to include the classification of nutrients and their role in human physiology. But it was not until the 20th century that scientists identified human nutritional requirements and the amino acids, vitamins, fatty acids, and minerals essential to the human diet.

After World War II, the major focus of attention in nutrition shifted from acute nutrient deficiency to chronic degenerative diseases such as heart disease, cancer, and diabetes, as nutrition scientists began to examine the relationship of modern dietary patterns and practices to these chronic diseases. The computer made possible extensive biochemical, epidemiological, and dietary intake studies that established mathematical correlates between dietary intake and health outcomes. In 1971, the Department of Health and Human Services (DHHS) undertook the first National Health and Nutrition Examination Survey, which became part of what is called the National Nutrition Monitoring System—a complex assessment of interconnected activities that regularly provides quantitative data about dietary intake and the nutritional habits of the American people and about factors that affect diet and nutritional status.

As a result of the greatly expanded research made possible by the computer, there was a decided shift in the Federal Dietary recommendations to the general public—a shift from recommendations for what people should include in their diets to what they should exclude. Since 1977, the Federal Government has been recommending that we limit our intake of sugar, fat, cholesterol, and salt, and since 1979, alcohol as well. Because the recommendations were backed by scads of tables, graphs, and figures on the health risks these foods caused, this flood of cautionary advice helped to deepen risk aversion in the society.

In addition to the health risks people face from ingesting natural foods like salt, sugar, and fats, the health danger establishment also began warning us in the 1970s about the hazards from manufactured products that contained cancer-causing chemicals. Since the early 1900s, scientists had suspected, on theoretical grounds, that industrial chemicals cause a large amount of cancer in human beings, but they had no scientific evidence to prove this. With the computer, however, they could establish correlations between chemicals and cancer. In the computer age, the Federal Drug Agency (FDA), together with newly created regulatory agencies like the Environmental Protection Agency (EPA), the Occupational Safety and Health Administration (OSHA), and the Consumer Product Safety Commission (CPSC), has issued warnings, based on quantitative analyses, about the potential threat to health and life of about 2,000 manufactured products and processes, In addition, the FDA has warned the public about the potential hazard of 10,000 food additives, and the EPA has reported that 35,000 pesticide formations are potentially hazardous.

One of the most prolific producers of statistics was the National Cancer Institute, whose quantitative studies sought to convince politicians and lay people that cancer was largely preventable. In October 1975, CBS produced a documentary entitled "The American Way of Death." Dan Rather opened the program by announcing that "the United States is number one in cancer." He went on to report that the National Cancer Institute estimates that "if you are living in America, your chances of getting cancer are higher than anywhere else in the world." The following year, Leslie Stahl, on the CBS documentary "The Politics of Cancer," reported that industry-related cancer rates were "soaring." In an NBC special produced in 1976, "What is This Thing Called Food?", Betty Furness reported that a calamity to the human species might be on its way: "Some scientists worry over the kind of safety tests being done today. They even talk about genetic disaster." That same year James Bishop, the national Energy and Environmental correspondent for *Newsweek*, relying on sources at the National Cancer Institute, told a "Face the Nation" audience that 60% to 90% of all known cancer is caused by man-made toxic chemicals of various sorts.

THE QUANTIFICATION OF ENVIRONMENTAL RISKS

Most commentators credit Rachel Carson's book, *The Silent Spring* (1962), with launching the modern environmental movement. I have argued elsewhere that more credit should be given to television than to any book (Perkinson, 1991). Here, I want to suggest that it was the quantification of potential and actual environmental disasters that made environmental risk credible to most Americans. Carson used some but not much quantification of actual environmental hazards in her book. The opening chapter, "A Fable for Tomorrow," was about an imaginary town—"that didn't exist, but ought to." In this imaginary town, a white granular powder (DDT?) killed the vegetation, destroyed the wildlife, and polluted the streams. Relying primarily on anecdotes and her lyrical prose, Carson did make readers suspect that pesticides were destroying the food chain and endangering all species, including the human species. Her book sparked groups like the Environmental Defense Fund to gather and process quantitative data on their computers that supported her claims. They publicized the numbers that revealed the decline in the bird population; the persistence of DDT in the bodies of birds, fish, and domestic animals; and the overall increase in cancer. Such quantification prompted the Environmental Protection Agency (EPA) in 1972 to ban all uses of DDT unless an essential public purpose could be proved.

The first environmental scientist to rely on and present quantitative data to make his case was population; the Paul Ehrlich, in his book, *The Population Bomb* (1968). "No matter how you slice it, population is a numbers game" (p. 17). The world population, he warned, is doubling every 37 years, which means that after a century it will have multiplied eight times. Overpopulation, he argued, poses a threat to human survival. First, there will not be enough food to feed everyone, causing widespread famine. Moreover, vast numbers of people will lead to more pollution and more depletion of the resources of the earth.

Ehrlich made a guest appearance on the Johnny Carson show in 1970, the first of several, where he captivated the audience with facts and figures about the coming apocalypse. Ehrlich's book sold 3 million copies and became the basis for national and international efforts at family planning.

Ehrlich seems not to have used a computer in his analysis, relying instead on the population figures compiled by the United Nations. But a few years later the center for the study of environmental risks shifted to MIT, and the computer became central to all analyses.

At MIT, a group of 40 scholars and scientists used computer simulation to produce a study entitled, "Man's Impact on the Global Environment (1970)." Although they complained of a lack of data, the group used what was available to generate numbers and figures that provided a rationale for warnings against DDT and the proposed Supersonic Transport (SST). Two years later, a second MIT computer study appeared, called *Limits to Growth* (Meadows, Meadows, Randers, & Behren, 1972). Using numbers to indicate the population of the world, the amount of arable land, and the stock of unrenewable resources, they attempted to predict how those variables would change in the course of time. The numbers the computer came up with showed that the population crisis, the food crisis, and the natural resources crisis would interact and peak, possibly in 30 years, producing the collapse of civilization and human death on an inconceivable scale. *Limits to Growth* sold 4 million copies.

In his book, *The Closing Circle* (1971), Barry Commoner challenged the simplistic notion that universal environmental pollution was due to an increase in population. He made a computer analysis of the rate of each production activity in the United States. First, he computed the average annual percentage change in production activity since 1949. Second, he computed the overall 25-year growth rates for each activity. By arranging these activities in decreasing order of growth rate, he produced a picture of how the United States economy had grown since World War II.

From this picture, Commoner concluded that, although production for most basic needs—food, clothing, housing—kept up with the 40% to 50% increase in population, the kinds of goods produced had changed drastically. Soap powder had been displaced by synthetic detergents; natural fibers replaced by synthetic ones; steel and lumber had given way to aluminum, plastics, and concrete; and synthetic insecticides (like DDT) had replaced older methods. What had changed, obviously, was the technology of production rather than the overall output of economic goods. This, Commoner concluded, is the source of most environmental pollution: "A good deal of the mystery and confusion about the sudden emergence of an environmental crisis can be removed by pinpointing, pollutant by pollutant, how the postwar technological transformation of the United States economy has produced not only the much-heralded 126 percent rise in the GNP, but also at a rate about ten times faster than the growth of the GNP, the rising level of environmental pollution (p. 146)."

The synthetic products of modern technology pollute the environment because they are not biodegradable, like detergents or plastics, or because they are biochemically active—like insecticides—and attack the nervous system of insects, as well as other organisms. In addition, the lead and nitrogen oxide emitted by technologically improved high-combustion automobiles pollute the air with smog.

Because our technological progress has been counter-ecological, Commoner insisted that we must change our production technology. During the 1970s, a risk-aversive society complied: Unleaded gas replaced leaded, new cars were equipped with catalytic converters, DDT was banned, and all detergents became biodegradable, as did many of the cartons, boxes, bags, and sacks used to package goods. Doing all this, the environmental establishment told us, was a matter of survival.

And if we are to survive, Commoner warned, "ecological considerations must guide economic and political ones (p. 292)." What this meant was that the environmental movement had to become a political movement. This did happen in 1980. In that year, Commoner ran for President of the United States as a candidate of the Citizens

Party, which he had founded, with a program of providing greater government control over industry for the sake of the environment.

The next large-scale computer analysis of the environment was conducted by the Federal government. In 1977, President Jimmy Carter commissioned the Council on Environmental Quality and the State Department to compile a report on the environment, which was published under the title, *Global 2000 Report to the President of the United States* (1980).

In the letter of transmittal, the Committee chairman pointed out that the report contained not predictions, but "projections developed by U.S. government agencies of what will happen to population, resources, and environment if present policies continue." The first two paragraphs of the Report summarized the committee's major findings and conclusions:

> If present trends continue, the world in 2000 will be more crowded, more polluted, less stable ecologically, and more vulnerable to disruption than the world we live in now. Serious stresses involving population, resources, and environment are clearly visible ahead. Despite material output, the world's people will be poorer in many ways than they are today.
>
> For hundreds of millions of the desperately poor, the outlook for food and other necessities of life will be no better. For many it will be worse. Barring revolutionary advances in technology, life for most people on earth will be more precarious in 2000 than it is now—unless the nations of the world act decisively to alter current trends.

More than 1 million copies of the original report have been distributed. *Time* and *Newsweek* ran full page stories and *Global 2000* made front-page newspaper headlines across the country as an "official" government study forecasting global disaster.

In compiling its report, the Committee used a computer "global model" constructed from three different models: a population model located in a computer in the Bureau of the Census; an energy model found in a computer in the Department of Energy; and a model for food in the computer used by the Department of Agriculture. These sector models were supplemented with additional data, outside contracts, and expert judgments. The Report conceded that this approach did lead to "inconsistencies and missing linkages that are unavoidable," but insisted that the numbers the global model came up with "understate the severity of potential problems the world will face as it prepares to enter the twenty-first century" (p. 7). The

Report recommended changes in national and international policies, more central planning, and world cooperation.

During the Reagan administration, *Global Report 2000* was largely ignored by the people Reagan appointed to head the EPA (Ann Gorsuch) and the Department of the Interior (James Watt). Both political appointees—neither of whom lasted through the entire administration—worked while they held those offices to *reduce* federal governmental environmental regulations.

During the Reagan administration, one very large computer-based environmental study was undertaken: the National Acid Precipitation Assessment Project (NAPAP), which involved over 2,000 scientists and an expenditure of over $500 million. The study concluded that an acid rain problem exists but claimed it is not as severe or urgent as many had feared. According to the Report, lake and stream acidity came not from precipitation but instead was overwhelmingly the product of the relative acidity and alkalinity of the local soils and rocks through which the ground water passed. The study found no evidence of widespread forest damage from acid rain. The damage that had been attributed to acid rain was actually the result of pests, diseases, and climactic stress, according to the report. But when the NAPAP report came out in 1990, the Congress and President Bush ignored it and adopted an acid rain program as part of the new Clean Air Act that cost an estimated $3 to $7 billion—most of which fell on midwestern and farm states.

The Clean Air Act of 1990 was the culmination of widespread concern about the greenhouse effect: Greenhouse gases are increasing in concentration and their many effects are threatening the planet. The greenhouse theory originated at the turn of the century with Swedish Nobel Laureate Svante Arrhenius, who contended that if we increase the amount of heat-trapping gasses, such as CO_2, in the atmosphere, the overall temperature of the earth will rise. As a result, forests will shift northward; sea levels will rise, causing floods; rainfall patterns will change; air pollution will worsen; and fires, draughts, and insect plagues will increase.

During the 20th century, the elaborate mathematical models used to conduct research on the climate response to the increase in CO_2 became increasingly intricate and complex. By the end of the 1960s, these models were put into computers and the research and analysis expanded. By the 1980s, leading computer modeling groups in the United States included the Geophysical Fluid Dynamics laboratory in New Jersey, the National Center for Atmospheric Research in Colorado, Oregon State University, and Goddard Institute for Space Studies in New York. All the climate models predict an increase in global temperatures as a doubling of CO_2 occurs. They differ, however, about the magnitude of the resultant warming. Moreover, not all scientists actively involved in global climate research believe that global warming has begun. (Only 17% do, according to a recent Gallup poll, whereas 30% say they do not know, and 53% do not believe that global warming has occurred.) Part of the uncertainty, as Robert Balling, Director of the Office of Climatology, has pointed out, after an extensive review of the computer models, is the fact that none of the models include the role of the ocean in absorbing CO_2 and in storing and transporting heat—which is something we do know affects climate warming (1992, pp. 34-46).

In spite of the present limitations on computing power and the limitations in our present state of knowledge about the physics of the atmosphere, two actual climactic events in 1988 and 1989 helped convince many people that global warming had already begun: Hurricane Gilbert in 1988 and hurricane Hugo in 1989 convinced many that the greenhouse theory was correct, because violent hurricanes ("hypercanes") were predicted by the climate models to be one of the consequences of global warming. In addition, the raging wildfires in Yellowstone Park during Summer 1988 were viewed as being in accord with predictions made by the computer climate models.

As a result, on November 15, 1990, President George Bush signed into law the Clean Air Act, which amended the original 1970 Clean Air Act and its amendments of 1977. This sweeping legislation tightened emission standards for industrial plants and automobiles, and at the same time established statutory deadlines by which cities had to attain the stringent ambient air quality standards mandated by this Act. In addition, the Act contained an alternative fuels program that set standards for the content and composition of motor fuels. Beginning in 1992, gasoline sold in cities that failed to attain the federal standards for carbon monoxide and ozone had to contain a minimum of 2% oxygen.

WHY THE QUANTIFICATION OF RISKS MAKE US RISK AVERSIVE

The science of risk analysis has made us aware of new risks we had not known about before. It has provided scientific-mathematical support for risks we had suspected existed. And it has elaborated the magnitude and incidence of risks of which we were already aware. More than this, the quantification of risks has reified the hazards humans face in a way that had never happened before: Quantification has made risks more credible. In this numerically saturated information environment, risk aversion is rational behavior.

Early on, people knew that some streams stank and could even catch fire, they realized that the air in some places was brown, and they were aware that some beaches were covered with waste and raw sewage. But they were not risk aversive. One investigator found that as late as 1963—before the widespread use of the computer and the avalanche of risk quantification—few people had stopped smoking, taken a polio vaccine, or started using seatbelts in their cars, despite all the information in the mass media about lung cancer, polio, and traffic accidents (Robinson, 1963). But through the quantitative analyses made possible by the computer, scientists have been able to ascertain ratios, such as parts per million concentrations of pollution in the air; they have been able to ascertain quantities, such as how many tons of sewage were dumped on to a beach, or how much effluent was released into the water, how much soil was contaminated; and they have come up with mathematical probabilities, such as how many cases of sickness and death would probably result from each hazard we face.

Now, it is true, as Stephen Jay Gould argued, that accepting any claim only because it is backed by copious numbers constitutes a profound misunderstanding of science (Gould, 1981). Nevertheless, this *is* how most of us do react: We believe that quantified data gives any claim scientific validity, conferring on it a kind of unassailability. This is borne out by a survey Cynthia Crossen commissioned the Gallup organization to conduct, which found that 82% of the American public said "statistics increased a story's credibility" (1994, p. 36).

So, my suggestion is that the computer has helped us to become a risk-aversive society. Inundated with the probabilities of risk, with graphs, figures, and charts that depict the average number of deaths, illnesses, and other hazards to our well-being and to our way of life, we have understandably become more risk aversive. All our diurnal activities—breathing, eating, drinking, traveling, not to mention smoking—seem fraught with quantifiable risks.

It is not just the plethora of statistics, charts, and graphs that have made us risk aversive. More to the point is that the arguments of the risk analysts are irrefutable. That is, none of us can disprove these risks exist, especially because risk analysts present them as mathematical probabilities. Moreover, the risk analyst can always find scientific, quantifiable evidence for any supposed risk. What is not a risk when a parts-per-million test can always be exposed to a parts-per-billion examination. If rats cope with a heavy dose of a chemical soaked into their food and water, one can always increase the dose. Or try mice or rabbits (Clarke, 1980).

The risk analyst has no stopping rule, other than the sought-for effect, so there is no possible way to refute his or her claim that a risk exists. Risk analysts operate like the Inquisitors of the 17th century who asked the accused if she was a witch: If she said no, what else would one expect of a witch? So, she was tortured until she confessed the truth. Under the guise of ascertaining who was a witch, the Inquisition simply promoted the belief that there were more witches than people ever realized. Similarly risk analysts, under the guise of ascertaining what risks exist, might simply be promoting the belief that there are more risks than people ever realized.

Although quantification makes risks more credible, at the same time it makes us more uncertain about them. This happens because we all know it is difficult for anyone to estimate what might happen in the future: We know that we can never think of everything that could possibly happen. We know there is also the human factor—that is, we can never predict how someone will behave in a given situation. And we know that events do not always occur in an expected, neat, order. So when we are given a quantified probable risk assessment—say the probability of an accident at a nuclear power plant, or the probability that a chemical food additive will cause cancer, or the probability that a defective part in an automobile will cause an accident—we become more uncertain: uncertain about both the assigned probability that the event will occur, and uncertain about the anticipated probable consequences of the event.

Such uncertainty usually leads us to believe that the risk in question is greater than the risk analysts say it is. And when, as often happens, the media take up this matter, they conduct polls about people's opinions about the risk probability. Inevitably, public opinion is that the risk probability is greater than what the experts tell us. Newspapers, magazines, and television news shows then give equal weight to such public opinion, which further increases risk aversion in the society.

What do we do about risk? Each person's reaction to the ceaseless and unending statistics about risks to our health, safety, and to the environment depends on his or her habitual way of life—the ideology he or she lives by (Douglas & Wildavsky, 1982; Wildavsky, 1991). Those who are *fatalists* tend to avoid and ignore statistics about risk because this enables them not to worry over things they believe they can do nothing about: What you don't know can't hurt you. Others, usually called *individualists*, accept risks as a part of life, the price one pays for progress and improvement. Confident in human rationality, they expect human inventiveness to be able to overcome or mitigate risks in the long run. A third group, who can be called *hierarchists*, retain a strong faith in experts, expecting them to make the right decisions about risk assessment and risk management. A fourth group, the *egalitarians*, not only accepts the reality and immanence of statistically described risks, they also blame the system for imposing hidden, involuntary dangers on people.

This last group, the egalitarians, shares what I called, in Part One, the intellectual framework of postmodernism—the belief that we cannot know the truth about goings-on in the world and that, consequently, all claims to know the truth are simply attempts to control: Those with power impose their ideas on the rest of us. When one looks at our social, political, and economic institutions (the system) through the lens of this intellectual framework it becomes patently clear that those who have created and who man these institutions have imposed rules, policies, practices, and procedures on the rest of us that serve their own interests.

The way—perhaps the only way—to combat such oppression, the argument goes, is to create a more equal society—a society in which no one group will have power over others, and no one group is privileged. As I see it, the intellectual framework of postmodernism gives rise to the ideology of egalitarianism, and this ideology ignites and fuels the flames of risk aversion: No group, egalitarians declare, should be able to put others at risk.

The growth of the postmodern intellectual framework in the last 20 or 30 years has brought about an increase in the number of people who subscribe to the egalitarian ideology. It is the prevalence of this ideology that has determined society's reaction to risk—evident in the dramatic expansion of laws and policies, and court decisions enacted to regulate, control, and curtail how the system functions. This hostile interference with the existing social, political, and economic arrangements discredits the system and those who maintain it, thereby shoring up the egalitarian ideology.

What I am suggesting is that statistics about risks do not alone lead to societal measures to avert risks. It is only when the risks at issue are thought to be involuntary and irreversible *and* to be somehow caused by the system that those statistics lead to societal measures to manage or control risk.

Take smoking. We have had scads of statistical data demonstrating that smoking is dangerous to health. ("Smoking is the nation's leading cause of statistics," one wag noted.) Yet, little was done to discourage smoking, except affixing a small warning label on each pack of cigarettes. It was only with the discovery of the phenomenon of secondary smoke that we had the enactment of prohibitions against smoking. Secondary smoke puts nonsmokers at risk. Because this is a nonvoluntary risk, it is only fair, the egalitarians argue, to set up social measures to curtail or eliminate smoking.

But there is more to the egalitarian analysis. The attack on smoking is at the same time an attack on the tobacco industry, one of the bastions of the economic system. Hence the readiness of egalitarians to ban smoking wherever possible. Compare this to the war on drugs. We have an abundance of statistics demonstrating the danger of drugs to health and safety, and there is much statistical evidence that drug addiction creates dangers and involuntary risk for the families, neighbors, and co-workers of the addict. But, although we do have laws against drugs, drug taking is endemic in society, and social measures against drugs have been relatively weak (admonitions like, "Just say no"). Whereas many stores, restaurants, offices, and entire buildings have signs declaring that they are smoke-free areas, it is only at schools that one sees signs announcing that the area is a drug-free zone.

I suggest that social measures against drugs have been relatively weak, compared to social measures against smoking, because attacks on drugs, unlike attacks on smoking, are not attacks on the system. Unlike smoking, people do not know why so many take drugs: There is no one to blame. Indeed, many egalitarians advocate the legalization of drugs: This *is* an attack on the system. And this is what egalitarians are about: attacking the system because it does not provide equal protection to all.

6

PROFESSIONAL RISK MANAGEMENT

As society has become more risk aversive it has turned to the government—to the federal regulatory agencies, congress, and the courts—to manage risk.

In the 1970s, Congress passed a slew of laws that assigned the task of risk management to existing and newly created regulatory agencies. These included:

Poison Prevention Packaging Act (1970)
Amended Federal Hazardous Substance Act (1970)
Clean Air Act Amendments (1970)
Occupational Safety and Health Act (1970)
Federal Boat Safety Act (1971)
Amended National Traffic & Motor Vehicle Safety Act (1972)
Technology Assessment Act (1972)
Drug Listing Act; Amended Federal Food, Drug and Cosmetic Act (1972)
Federal Insecticide, Fungicide and Rodenticide Act (1972)
Consumer Product Safety Act (1972)
Safe Drinking Water Act (1974)
Amended Federal Insecticide, Fungicide and Rodenticide Act (1976)

Amended Public Health Service Act (1976)
National Consumer Health Information and Health
Promotion Act (1976)
Toxic Substance Control Act (1976)

QUANTIFICATION AND ITS PROBLEMS

The 1976 Toxic Substance Control Act was hastened by the announcement by Russell Train, head of the Environmental Protection Agency (EPA), that America was being assaulted by 2,000,000 toxic chemicals. (Two years later, Joseph Califano, Secretary of Health, Education, and Welfare (HEW), raised the number to 7,000,000.) But once the Act was passed, it revealed the magnitude of the problem of risk management through regulation.

When they set out to assess the carcinogenicity of chemicals by analyzing the risk to animals, the regulatory scientists discovered there were not enough toxicologists, nor sufficient laboratories to test the 50,000 or 60,000 industrial compounds that existed, not to mention the estimated 1,000 new compounds that appeared every year. Moreover, each animal test was expensive—as much as $50,000 for one unreplicated test—and it took three years to execute.

In addition to the practical problems of testing toxic chemical compounds, the regulatory scientists confronted methodological criticisms of their work. Some critics argued that mice may be 3×10^4 to 10^9 times more prone to cancer than humans, so they reject extrapolations of the results from animals to humans, as well as the extrapolation from the high doses given to mice to the low doses humans experience. Indeed, critics point out that different mathematical models for extrapolating from high dose exposures to low-dose exposures produce estimated cancer rates that can differ by factors of 1,000 or more at the expected levels of human exposure.

In addition, critics have claimed that the difficulties in estimating synergistic effects (interactions between two or more substances, e.g., between cigarette smoking and exposure to asbestos) and effects on particularly sensitive people (e.g., children, pregnant women, the elderly) further compound the problem of risk assessment (Covello, 1986). One of the critics, writing in *Science*, in 1980, concluded: "Discouraging as it may seem, it is not plausible that animal carcinogenesis experiments can be improved to the point where quantitative generalizations about human risk can be drawn from them" (Bori, 1980, p. 261).

Although the risk-management establishment had become hobbled by impracticable goals and constrained by methodological obstacles, the only way out seemed to be more quantification: better identified goals and more defensible standards. This proved fruitless.

During the high tide of health, safety, and environmental legislation in the 1970s, both the legislators and the public assumed that the federal regulatory agencies would be able to establish definite zero risk levels of exposure to health hazards. Earlier, in 1959, an even more naive Congress had passed the Delany Act, which set a limit of zero at any dosage for the amount of any food, drug, or cosmetic additive that had shown any evidence of causing cancer in man or animals, at any dosage. Since no scientist would ever maintain that any additive contains zero risk (you cannot prove a negative), it is logically impossible to enforce such a law. Moreover, even if the regulatory agency were to pursue the "softer" policy of eliminating risks up to the capacity of available technology, to do so would be economically disastrous. There is always a technology conceivable that is an improvement on a previous one—but as the last increment of risk is removed, the cost of each successive fix goes up: Technology A allows a residual risk of 10^6 and costs $1 million; technology B allows a residual risk of 10^{60} and costs $10 million, and on and on, and up and up, it goes.

If there can be no zero-risk exposure level, and we cannot financially afford to eliminate every identified risk, then what is a regulatory agency to do? "How safe is safe enough?" became the central question for risk managers.

The answer, according to the regulatory scientists, was the quantification of acceptable risk. In 1969, Chauncey Starr, who was then head of the nuclear reactor division of North American Aviation, presented an approach for establishing a quantitative measure of benefits relative to costs "for accidental deaths arising from technological developments in public use" (Starr, 1969, p. 1232). Pointing out that the history of technological growth demonstrates that people are willing to undergo the costs it entails because of the benefits it brings, he suggested that "if we understood quantitatively the causal relationships between specific technological developments and societal value, both positive and negative, we might deliberately guide and regulate technological development so as to achieve maximum social benefit at minimal social cost" (p. xx). This, Starr said, would provide a rough answer to the question: "How safe is safe enough?"

From his analysis, Starr drew the conclusion that the public will accept risks for voluntary activities, such as skiing, that are roughly a thousand times as great as it would tolerate from involuntary hazards, such as food preservatives that provide the same level of benefits.

Subsequent cost-benefit analysts found that voluntary exposure versus involuntary exposure was not the only mediator of risk acceptance. They found that people are not only more aversive to risks that are involuntary rather than voluntary, but they are also more aversive when the risks are catastrophic rather than chronic, total rather than just injurious, and new rather than old; people are also more aversive when the risks are not known rather than known, and not controllable rather than controllable. These psychological factors became the focus of numerous psychometric studies that employed quantitative methodologies to predict when a risk would be acceptable to the public (Covello, 1986).

But the risk managers soon discovered that the mathematical cost-benefit analysis of risk only made people more risk aversive. It is probably true that most of us do engage in rough-and-ready cost-benefit analysis in many of the decisions we have to make. (Is it worth going five miles farther to shop in a supermarket where we can save fifty cents on special sales?) But when the costs and benefits about matters of life and death or health and safety are presented to us in mathematical terms, this itself automatically makes us anxious and more risk aversive.

Moreover, the quantification of risk acceptability has made actual hazardous events seem worse than they are. That is, both risk-assessment and risk-acceptability studies have primed the public to anticipate such an event which leads us, when it happens, to perceive it as more severe than it actually is. And then we blame the risk managers for not adequately protecting people. Thus, when the nuclear fiasco occurred at Three Mile Island—where there was not a single fatality—many people construed this as a terrible event that showed that the nuclear experts had gone too far, had failed to take account of human operator error and incompetence, had come within a hair's breadth of totally losing control of the machine, and had at last given the nation reason to close down the entire nuclear industry.

Finally, quantification has increased the disputes among scientists about risk acceptability. In the case of radon, for example, the National Council on Radiation Protection recommends that action be taken at 8 picocuries per liter rather than the 4 picocuries per liter recommended by the Environmental Protection Agency, whereas scientists working for the Department of Energy have said that the risk of exposure to less than 10 picocuries per liter is merely comparable to the risks people normally accept in their lives and less than the risk of driving a car. In the face of such disagreements among experts over the numbers, what is the public to think? Such scientific controversy can only increase the public's distrust of experts. And because the experts are part of the system, such distrust shores up the egalitarian's hostility to the system.

So, as we increase the number of laws and regulations intended to manage risk, and scientists attempt to quantify risk acceptability, we find that risk aversion becomes institutionalized, transforming our society into one that is permanently risk aversive.

FURTHER ATTACKS ON THE SYSTEM

As more and more people became more aware of risks to their health and safety—risks caused by the "system"—many began to fight back. So, the growth of risk aversion has led to the litigation explosion. In this risk-aversive society, almost every industry has been the target of liability suits: prescription drugs, vaccines, contraceptives, sporting equipment, and automobile manufacturers; and the manufacturers of tools, appliances, factory machinery, chemicals, children's wear, and materials-handling equipment. According to Peter Huber (1988), cases in which appliances, factory machinery, chemicals, automobiles, and other products were blamed for injuries increased four-fold between 1976 and 1986. More medical malpractice suits were filed in the decade ending in 1987 than ever before. By 1985, one out of four obstetrician-gynecologists had been sued. There was also an increase in the damage claims against cities—these doubled between 1982 and 1986—as well as against the Federal Government. Everywhere people were attacking the system.

Yet, it is not the explosion in litigation itself that is so remarkable but the fact that most court decisions have gone against business and industry, against the government, against medical experts. The courts have agreed that in most instances the system is at fault.

Some of these claims were class action suits, the most famous being the Agent Orange suit against seven chemical companies and the U.S. Government, which comprised 600 separate suits, representing 2.4 million people directly or indirectly affected by the millions of tons of Agent Orange (which contained traces of dioxin) sprayed by U.S. forces in the Vietnam War to destroy enemy cover. In May 1984, the veterans settled this claim against the seven chemical companies for $180 million.

In response to the risk-aversive sentiments coursing through the country, federal and state legislatures have enacted legislation that facilitates attacks on the system through the courts. Congress and state legislatures have passed new rules that relax the admissibility of evidence, thereby allowing plaintiffs (and defendants) to bring in special experts—physicians, psychologists, chemists, engineers, and statisticians of all varieties. Companies have actually emerged that offer to supply experts to testify on behalf of lawyer's clients for a fee. One area where experts were widely used by plaintiffs' lawyers was the so-called bad-baby suits. Here, lawyers found experts who would testify that birth-deformed babies were caused by contraceptives, or by medicines, or vaccines administered during pregnancy; some experts blamed the obstetrician for fetal asphyxiation during labor. The manufacturers of the drug, *Bendectine,* prescribed safely for decades against morning sickness in pregnancy, suffered so many suits that it finally pulled the drug off the market. This, despite the fact that the FDA, and virtually all researchers, rejected the claim that *Bendectine* caused birth defects.

Some states passed right-to-sue laws that allowed any citizen (usually a lawyer, it turned out) to sue anyone who failed to comply with one or another part of some vast body of federal litigation. (Some recently passed federal statutes also include explicit provision for citizen suits.) At the same time, many states threw out time and space limitations, which increased the likelihood that a person could be sued at any time and any place. In 1981, for example, Mrs. Earl Cowan, whose husband had been hurt in an automobile accident in Texas five years before, filed a suit against Ford Motor Company in Mississippi—not Texas—because the statute of limitations had run out in Texas.

The most important legal changes that have made it possible to attack the system through the courts have been the ones that have taken place in tort law (the law of personal injury) in the last 30 years. Most significant has been the abandonment of the necessity of demonstrating negligence in personal injury suits and its replacement with the concept of strict liability, that is liability regardless of fault. Strict liability has been extended to products (called *product liability*) through the notion that manufacturers are responsible for making products safe for any "reasonable foreseeable use." Under this dictum, one manufacturer was held liable for damages because of a failure to warn purchasers of special "baseball sunglasses" that if a baseball struck them going full force, they could crack. In 1980, a court ruled that a pajama manufacturer should pay damages for not doing more to make pajamas flame resistant.

The most clear evidence that the litigation explosion has become an all-out attack on the system is the dramatic rise in punitive damage awards. Before the 1970s, only about 0.5% of all tort claims filed against the Ford Motor Company asked for punitive damages; by 1975, such demands had risen ten-fold, and by 1980 punitive damages were being sought in a quarter of all cases. Manufacturers of contraceptives almost never faced punitive damage awards until the Dalkon Shield came along. In 1975, S.H. Robbins, manufacturer of the shield, had to pay $75,000 in punitive damages, and by July 1985, 11 juries had awarded a total of $24.8 million in punitive damages, while pending suits were demanding at least another $12 billion in punishment. The Dalkon Shield was taken off the market, but it opened the floodgates for punitive attacks on safer substitutes: Ortho Pharmaceutical Corporation was slapped with a $2.75 million punitive award (on top of $2 million in compensation) in a "failure to warn" lawsuit involving the pill; and a $5.1 million punitive award was levied against the maker of a widely used spermicidal gel. In another punitive damage case, the Sabin polio vaccine, strongly endorsed by public health authorities, had a string of victories in liability cases, with some scattered defeats; then in June 1984, ran into a $10 million verdict, $8 million of it in punitive damages Olson, 1981).

One result of the attacks on the system by this phenomenal number of liability cases has been the increase in the amount of insurance carried by corporations, cities, and individual professionals. At one time, doctors, but not many other professionals, had to worry about buying malpractice insurance. Now others worry, too: nurses, amateur sports umpires, hairdressers, and veterinarians. But as the liability cases increased and the awards got larger and larger, the insurance companies began to raise their rates dramatically and, in some cases, backed out completely. As the insurance companies saw it, there was no way to insure against the misdeeds of obstetricians, drug companies, or hazardous waste companies if these agents were to be charged at unpredictable intervals for diseases and accidents that they had not in fact caused.

As insurance rates soared, or dried up entirely, obstetricians began refusing new patients; some stopped practicing altogether. Contraceptive manufacturers, finding no insurance available, discontinued their products. Most of the country's large consulting-engineering firms found it impossible to get pollution liability insurance and began refusing to handle toxic waste sites.

Toxic waste became increasingly worrisome to people as government agencies generated more and more fearsome numbers. In 1980, the EPA estimated that Americans produced more than 57 million metric tons of hazardous waste per year. In 1983, the Office of Technology Assessment set this figure at 255-275 million tons. The director of the Office of Solid Waste of the EPA claimed that over 750,000 businesses generated hazardous waste, and over 10,000 transporters moved these wastes for treatment or disposal to over 30,000 sites.

All these fearsome figures, coupled with the dramatic toxic spills at Love Canal in New York State and in other sites around the nation, further discouraged the private sector—the hazardous waste companies and the insurance companies—from trying to deal with such risks. As a result the Federal Government stepped in by passing the Environmental Response, Compensation, and Liability Act (CER-CLA), or "Superfund" as it came to be called. This made matters worse, by deepening and strengthening hostility to the "system"—hostility now directed at the government experts.

Under Superfund, first enacted in 1980 and amended in 1986, the polluters were liable for all toxic waste removal. Those who fell under the label of polluters included: prior owners of a damaged site, users, bankers, insurers, waste generators, and transporters. Moreover, a generator of waste could be held liable even if there was no direct link between the specific waste he contributed to the site and the harm that occurred. It was enough to show that the site caused harm and that he contributed waste to that site. Further any liable party could be held responsible for the entire clean-up settlement regardless of how small his portion of responsibility.

The potential economic costs to any firm caught in this net of liability has resulted in endless court battles to wiggle free or drag others into the net. In an effort to clean up a site near Utica, New York, the EPA sued two companies—a cosmetic producer and a manufacturer of metal components. They, in turn, sued over 600 mostly small businesses and 41 towns and school districts—including a pizzeria, whose trash, the attorney for the two large companies surmised, "might have included empty cleanser or insecticide cans containing trace amounts of toxins" (Landy & Hague, 1992, p. 100). Moreover, because the cost of treatment is free to the local communities and the waste treatment companies, they insist on "permanent treatment" of each site. This makes the task even more costly, and possibly endless.

After one decade, Superfund yielded little in the way of site clean-up and it has produced an economic and legal morass that drains a lot of public and private money, much of which goes to the special interests—lawyers and waste treatment companies—who dominate Superfund policies. A Rand Corporation study showed that about 80% of the money spent on Superfund has gone to pay lawyer's fees. Only 109 hazardous waste sites (out of 1,200 identified by the EPA) have been cleaned up at a cost of $15 billion.

THE DESTABILIZATION OF SOCIETY

The quantification of risk has undoubtedly made our society more risk aversive. People have become more cautious in their habits and their life styles, becoming thereby healthier and safer. In October 1990, *The New York Times* reported that fatal accidents in the last decade had declined 21%. In December 1994, the Center for Disease Control and Prevention reported that average life expectancy had risen to an all time high of 75.8 years and that death rates for heart disease, cancer, stroke, lung disease, accidents and pneumonia-influenza had all dropped between 1979 and 1992.

But efforts to manage risk aversion have weakened and destabilized society by provoking hostility toward the government, toward industry and business, and toward professionals like physicians and lawyers. This hostility has in turn evoked counterproductive behavior from manufacturers and physicians. Physicians prescribe too many tests, and manufacturers add too many safety features—often based on reference to what a jury can be made to believe rather than what is actually safest. This saps and diverts resources, as well as increases costs—thereby making many products, and medical care, too, unaffordable to lower income people: They do without, or in the case of products, continue to use older, less safe, substitutes.

Moreover, attempts to manage risk aversion have dampened innovation in many health and safety fields. Research expenditures by U.S. companies working on contraceptives peaked in 1973 and plummeted 99% in the next decade. "Who in his right mind," the president of a major pharmaceutical company asked in 1986, "would work on a product today that would be used by pregnant women?" (cited in Huber, 1988, p. 155). This has also happened in the case of vaccines: Between 1965 and 1985, the number of U.S. vaccine manufacturers declined by more than half, and today only two major companies are still investing heavily in vaccine research.

So, although heightened risk aversion, generated by the computer, has brought about a society more concerned about health and safety, the attempts to manage risks have impaired the health care system and weakened public confidence in health experts. Similarly, computer-generated heightened risk aversion has reduced environmental hazards: We have less pollution, more conservation of resources, and more family planning. But our attempts to manage risk have further destabilized society by politicizing the environmental movement. This has resulted in counterproductive measures that serve special interests at the expense of the public interest.

The use of computer models to make predictions about the future of the environment have been criticized ever since the publication of *Limits to Growth* (Meadows et al., 1972). Of that study, Nobel prize winner Gunnar Myrdal, wrote:

> The use of mathematical equations and a huge computer, which registers the alternative of abstractly conceived policies by a 'world simulation model' may impress the innocent general public, but has little, if any, scientific validity. That this sort of model is actually a new tool for mankind, is unfortunately not true. It represents quasi-learnedness of a type that we have, for a long time had too much of. (1973, pp. 70-71)

But, in spite of such criticisms, the use of computers by the environmental disaster establishment has made a strong impact on society.

I think this has happened because such studies rest on fundamental mathematical truths about the environment: It is true that there are population limits—a numerical limit to how many people the earth can support; it is also true that our natural resources are finite—there is a quantitative limit to what we can extract from the earth; and, it is true that there is a quantitative limit to the amount of pollution and waste the environment can absorb.

Yet, although it is true that there are mathematical limits, we do not know what those mathematical limits are. The leaders of the environmental movement refuse to live with this uncertainty and insist that we must act now—even if we do not know if human beings and the planet truly are at risk. The following are some quotes compiled by Dixie Lee Ray (1990, p. 167) from members of the environmental disaster establishment:

- An EPA panel on acid rain set up by William Ruckelshaus in 1983 reported: "If we take the conservative point of view that we must wait until the scientific knowledge is definitive, the accumulated deposition and damaged environment may reach the point of irreversibility."
- Jonathan Schell, author of *Our Fragile Earth*: "Now, in a widening sphere of decisions, the costs of error are so exorbitant that we need to act on theory alone, which is to say on prediction alone. It follows that the reputation of scientific prediction needs to be enhanced. But that can happen, paradoxically, only if scientists disavow the certainty and precision that they normally insist on. Above all, we need to learn to act decisively to forestall predicted perils, even while knowing that they may never materialize. We must

take action, in a manner of speaking, to preserve our ignorance. There are perils that we can be certain of avoiding
only at the cost of never knowing with certainty that they
were real."
- Richard Benedick, an employee from the State Department,
working on assignment for the Conservative Foundation:
"A global climate treaty must be implemented even if there
is no scientific evidence to back the greenhouse effect."
- Stephen Schneider, proponent of the theory that CFCs are
depleting the ozone: "We have to offer up scary scenarios,
make simplified, dramatic statements, and make little
mention of any doubts we may have. Each of us has to
decide what the right balance is between being effective
and being honest."

Although they have relied on computers to make their case
for managing risk by acting now, the numbers, graphs, and tables
generated by computers can only establish trends—growth in the
consumption of resources, growth in population, growth in pollution.
They can never demonstrate that we are approaching the mathematical limits. This is the argument made by many economists, especially Julian Simon. Simon argues that the ultimate resource is the
human mind. So the more people we have on this earth, the more
mind power we have to prevent the depletion of resources and to
diminish pollution of the environment. When the demand for a
resource exceeds the present supply, this leads to improved technology, which increases the supply, Simon argues. He goes so far as to
suggest that because the human mind can continually improve our
methods of extracting, processing, and/or synthesizing natural
resources, we actually will never run out of them. He points to the
continuous decline this in century in the prices of all natural minerals as corroboration of this (Simon, 1981).

But the arguments of Simon and others have been ignored by
the environmental disaster establishment in their determination to
manage risks by acting now. To *act now* means to establish government regulations that mandate and control activities that adversely
affect the environment. Who else but the government has the power
and the resources to eliminate environmental hazards? However, one
of the consequences of this centralized mandate and control approach
has been the politicization of the environmental movement. As a
result, the legislation passed by Congress usually winds up serving
special interests instead of the public interest. The Clean Air Act presents a paradigm case.

The original 1970 Clean Air Act served the interests of the American automobile manufacturers insofar as it, for all practical purposes, prohibited a type of air-cooled engine used by a foreign manufacturer—Volkswagen. As result, that technology disappeared from the American market after 1974. The 1977 Act incorporated the "clean coal/dirty air" deal between the high-sulfur coal producers and the environmentalists. The Clean Air Amendment Act of 1990 contained the alternative fuel provision that served the interests of midwestern farmers by all but mandating that ethanol (made from corn) was the only acceptable alternative fuel. This financial windfall for the entire midwest was in part retribution for the financial burdens imposed on that region by the acid rain provisions of the same act (Yardley, 1992).

Another example of how politicization of the environmental movement serves special interests is the just discussed Superfund, set up by the Federal government in 1980 to finance the clean-up of toxic waste sites. This act has benefited the environmental lawyers and the waste clean-up business, both of whom succeeded in fashioning an act that insisted on permanent treatment and "Cadillac clean" quality standards, thereby insuring continuous litigation and a nearly endless clean-up operation at each waste site. But it also insured that only a small number of sites would be cleaned.

One of the most distinctive features of Federal environmental legislation is the inclusion of a provision for "citizen suits." This allows "any citizen," or "any person" to sue private parties for compliance with the environmental statute. On the face of it, a provision for "citizen suits" seems far removed from politicization. But, in point of fact, this provision has resulted in the creation of an entitlement program for environmental groups.

"Citizen suits" are almost always brought by nationally organized professional advocacy groups, such as the Sierra Club Legal Defense Fund, or the National Resources Defense Council. Other national groups who initiate such suits include the Atlantic States Legal Foundation, the Public Interest Research Group, and the Friends of the Earth. In these suits, these groups recover attorney's fees from the defendants for educational and research programs. These fees can range from a few thousand to millions of dollars in a single case. Often, the environmental group threatens the target—usually a large corporation—with an expensive legal suit and then offers to settle the matter for a smaller sum—to be paid to the environmental group or cause.

One analysis of 29 cases between 1983 and 1988 showed that "more than 65 percent of the settlements, totaling slightly under $1,000,000, went to environmental groups" (Greve & Smith, 1992, p.

110). Another analysis of 30 Clean Water Act citizen suits against alleged polluters in Connecticut between 1983 and 1986 showed that the total settlement of more than $1.5 million included $492,036 in attorney's fees to the National Defense Council and the Connecticut Fund for the Environment (Greve & Smith, 1992).

Both Congress and the EPA recognize that the citizen suit provisions of environmental litigation do more to secure funding for environmental causes than they do to reduce pollution, but they defend it as "public participation." In reality, of course, as in other attempts of the Federal government to mandate and control for the public interest, this ends up expanding the opportunities for private groups to pursue their special interests.

Like the health danger establishment, the environmental danger establishment has bombarded us with computer-generated numbers that have increased our awareness of risk. Our attempts to avert risks through increased regulation and controls have made us a healthier and safer society. Risk management has also reduced environmental hazards: We have less pollution, more conservation of resources, and more family planning.

However, as I have tried to show, these efforts to avert risk have sprung from an ever-spreading and ever-deepening egalitarian ideology that blames all risks on the "system." Moreover, these egalitarian-inspired efforts to insure that all people are equally protected against risks by mandating regulation and control have provoked the wrath of both individualists and hierarchs. Individualists protest the loss of individual liberty when the government imposes regulations and controls. Hierarchs are dismayed by the fact that the conduct of the experts in the matter of risk management does not promote the public interest.

So, at the same time that we and our environment have become healthier and safer, we have all become more hostile to the "system"—more suspicious and antagonistic toward our government, our economic institutions, and our professional experts.

7

RISK-AVERSIVE GROUPS

So far, I have argued that the computer has helped make people risk aversive by generating statistics that revealed hitherto unknown risks to health, safety, and the environment. These risks affect everyone. The computer has also generated statistics that reveal that specific groups within the society are at risk. Blacks, women, the disabled, as well as homosexuals, ethnic minorities, the elderly, and children, are all groups who are not equally protected in the society: They are at risk.

The computer-generated statistics that demonstrated how much these groups are at risk not only galvanized the victims to secure equal protection, but it also enlisted advocates who supported their cause. These statistics had the greatest impact on those who were already inclined to an egalitarian ideology. The statistics reinforced the belief that the society itself was unfair and unequal.

Because the logic of the situation is the same, the attempts to manage group risk aversion have followed the same route as that taken in the management of health, safety, and environmental risks: following an avalanche of statistics about risk, which provoked a lot of hostility against the system, risk managers enacted measures to control risks by transforming the existing social arrangements. These actions further destabilized the society.

A WAR OF NUMBERS

Over the last two or three decades computers have compiled extensive statistical evidence that demonstrates how society puts some
groups at risk by failing to protect them and their rights. (See, for
example, Hacker's analysis of the 1980 Census [1983] and his study
of black and white America [1992]; Roberts's analysis of the 1990
Census [1993], and The Universal Almanac, published annually).

No one can, or does, dispute the now-familiar numbers that
prove that, compared to whites, a higher percentage of blacks live in
poverty; that blacks have fewer years of schooling, lower academic
grades, and a higher dropout rate; that there are more arrests of
blacks than whites, more criminal convictions, more incarcerations,
and more executions; that unemployment is higher among blacks,
and wages are lower; and that life expectancy for blacks is lower than
for whites, and infant mortality is higher.

The magnitude of the differences in life chances between
blacks and whites, and its persistence over generations, clearly
shows that as a group, black people are more at risk in this society
than white people.

The numbers reveal a similar picture of women in compari-
son with men. No one disputes the now-familiar statistics that prove
that female wages are lower than male wages; that fewer women
hold managerial or professional positions; that women are sexually
harassed and physically abused more than men; that teachers, physicians, and employers generally treat women differently from men.
Here, too, then, the persistent differences in life chances show that
women are more at risk in this society than men.

Similar statistical evidence has proven that homosexuals, the
disabled, and ethnic minorities suffer the same victimization in
employment, schooling, and health care.

These incontrovertible numbers, documenting how much at
risk some groups of people are, has weakened the faith of many in
the society. Confronted with these statistics, many have concluded
that discrimination is systemic. They argue that our political, social,
and economic arrangements embody the belief that some groups are
inferior: that blacks, women, homosexuals are not as smart, or not as
competent, or not as moral, as the rest of us. These embodied beliefs,
the critics maintain, allow the society to justify and legitimize the
unequal treatment these groups receive.

In response to these critics of the system, some point out that
the computer-generated statistics tell another story: Blacks, as a
group, during the last 20 or 30 years, have had more years of school-

ing and higher academic attainments; they have achieved a higher standard of living and improved medical care. The same holds true for women and homosexuals; They are now less discriminated against than ever before; they are less at risk. Indeed, the statistics show that in absolute terms ever since the end of World War II the life chances of all these groups have gotten better. It is only in the relative comparisons (blacks compared to whites, women compared to men, homosexuals compared to heterosexuals) that these groups come up as being at risk.

But why do we find more emphasis on relative deprivation than on the reduction of absolute deprivation? One explanation for this is the oft-cited Tocqueville effect. According to deTocqueville (Volume II, Book 2, chap. 13, 1805-1859), "The desire for equality always becomes more insatiable in proportion as equality is more complete." In other words, as inequalities diminish, the remaining inequalities become more unbearable. According to modern proponents of this theory, then, in the second half of the 20th century it was precisely because the condition of blacks, women, and homosexuals had improved that the remaining (relative) inequalities became so onerous to them and, therefore, the focus of complaint.

But there is another possible explanation for this focus on relative deprivation. The Tocqueville effect is a demand-side theory; that is, it asserts that it is those discriminated against, the victims, who demand more equality and more equal treatment. There is, however, a supply side theory that could also explain this phenomenon. That is, it could be that the increased supply of equality for these groups since the end of World War II has itself led to some of their number becoming more risk aversive. For increased equality (of opportunity) means the opportunity to fail as well as to succeed. So, as blacks, women, and homosexuals attained more equality they confronted the risk of failing. So some, rather than face the risk of failing, may have complained that they could not succeed because their condition was not yet equal to that of whites, or men, or heterosexuals.

Prior to this increase in equality (of opportunity) many, if not most, blacks, women, and homosexuals, understandably, subscribed to a fatalist ideology: One must accept the way things are; one cannot change the fact that in this society we do not have the same opportunities as whites, males, and heterosexuals. But as equality (of opportunity) increased over the years, fatalism no longer made sense. Now a woman, a black, or a homosexual, could become an autonomous individual, not simply a member of an oppressed group.

But the ideology of individualism carries risks that many find aversive. This is corroborated by a study of the 1944 all-female graduating class of Battin High School in Elizabeth, New Jersey.

According to a report in *The New York Times* (May 13, 1994), the women almost unanimously expressed an aversion to the risk of being responsible for their own conduct. In interviews they said that when they graduated from high school 50 years ago, they appreciated the security of the path that had awaited them—despite social limitations and close control by their parents. They would have been afraid to graduate today, when women have so many more opportunities. There is every reason to believe that most people, like them, would find it risky to face new opportunities not previously available.

No longer able to subscribe to a fatalistic ideology in a world of increased equal opportunity that had emerged since the end of World War II, those blacks, women, and homosexuals who are aversive to the risks entailed by taking up an individualist ideology have adopted the ideology of egalitarianism. Egalitarianism helps them make sense of and adapt to the changed world they now live in. According to this ideology, the system, no matter how much it has changed, remains inherently unequal, which means that it is impossible for blacks, women, and homosexuals to compete successfully until they have equality of condition with whites, men, and heterosexuals.

These two explanatory theories—the demand-side theory and the supply side theory—are not mutually exclusive. Undoubtedly, as Tocqueville suggests, for many blacks, women, and homosexuals, the demand for equality became more insatiable in proportion as equality became more complete. At the same time, for others, the increased supply of equality (of opportunity) may have elicited fear of the risk of failing; to avert failure they complained about their relative inequality of condition. But, in both cases—whether they wanted to avoid the risk of failure if they took advantage of the increased equality of opportunity, or whether they wanted to avoid the risk of discrimination that remained because of the absence of complete equality of opportunity—blacks, women, and homosexuals have become risk aversive. And in becoming risk aversive they blamed the system for denying them the same life chances accorded to others.

THE CHANGED LANGUAGE OF DISCOURSE

If the existing economic, social, and political arrangements put certain groups at risk, then people's consciousness had to be raised about the oppression inherent in the system. One way to do this was to talk about the system differently. Thus it happened that within a short period of time many were saying we live in a racist, sexist, and elitist society. One of the reasons Americans had not recognized this before was the long-standing belief that the status and condition of blacks, women, and homosexuals in the society were their own responsibility: The treatment they received was the treatment they deserved. The egalitarians rejected this long-standing belief, rejected it because it was nothing more than a case of blaming the victims for their own victimization.

To help change the status of the at-risk groups, the language of discourse employed new labels to replace those tainted with the stigma of inferiority: "Negro" and "colored" were replaced by "black" and, later, "African American;" "Mrs." and "Miss" gave way to "Ms", along with the abandonment of all gender-tinged words, such as "man" (for "person" or "human"). Along with the changes in labels came reconceptualizations of terms, such as homosexuality. Once, almost universally regarded as a sin, homosexuality now came to be spoken of as an alternative life style. (The only sin is the sinful discrimination against lesbians and gay men.)

Those at risk also succeeded in reconceptualizing the traditional family, characterizing it as a "patriarchical family," or sometimes as a "patriarchical proprietary family," because it construes the wife and children as the property of the husband/father. And abortion, once considered a crime, has become a right. While street crime, although still a crime, was now to be understood as "a reflection of a survival culture"—that is, behavior consciously propagated to neutralize the deleterious effects of institutionalized racism.

Not only were traditional labels changed and terms reconceptualized, but the meanings of some words were expanded to apply to situations and actions not covered before. Take "rape," for example. Some now argue that rape is a subjective experience, defined by the feelings of the person, not by physical assault or penetration (Sykes, 1992). Such expanded meanings serve to inflate the statistics on victimization. According to Catherine MacKinnon, Professor of Law at Michigan University: "Thirty-eight percent of us are raped in our marriages. Nearly half are victims of rape or attempted rape at least once in our lives, many more than once, especially women of color, many involving multiple attackers, mostly men we know. Eighty-five percent of women who work outside the home are sexually harassed at some point by employers" (1993, p. 7).

The term *sexual harassment* has undergone an expansion of coverage as seen in the 1993 survey by the American Association of University Women of public school children in grades 8 through 11. The survey found that 80% of all students in school claimed to be victims of sexual harassment. Examples of harassment in the survey included boys making catcalls, patting and pushing, and girls teasing other girls with childish sexual insults. Tellingly, 75% of the respondents who claimed harassment said that they did not tell a teacher, or even a parent.

The transformations in the language of discourse not only enable people to make sense of the computer-generated statistics about victimized groups, it also strengthens the belief that society itself is unfair and unjust and has to be changed radically.

In the next sections I focus primarily on the management of risks by blacks and women. Homosexuals comprise a special case in my argument, so I discuss them separately.

SOCIAL RECONSTRUCTION

To avert the risk of discrimination against them, advocates for blacks and women have secured new policies and practices in employment decisions, school admissions, health services, and other activities in which they are at risk. These include affirmative action, race norming, and disparate impact.

Critics (see, for example, Bovard, 1994; Hentoff, 1992; Magnet, 1993; Sykes, 1990, 1992; Taylor, 1992) complained that these policies and practices were not new, but simply new words for conduct that everyone had rejected in the past: affirmative action was nothing more than the insistence on quotas—racial or gender—in hiring or in school admissions; race norming was nothing more than using a double standard for evaluating whites and blacks; and disparate impact was simply an attempt to argue that racial- or gender-neutral treatment is actually discriminatory if the results adversely affect blacks or women—that is, if a company winds up hiring too few blacks or women, or a school admits too few, then the hiring policies or the admission policies are said to be discriminatory.

Critics go on to complain that the changes in social practices and social policies sought by these at-risk groups have not only introduced practices condemned as unacceptable in the past, but they also violate traditional principles, such as the presumption of innocence.

Consider the case of speech codes. *Hate speech* is defined as any words that create a hostile atmosphere or environment. In the 1980s a number of universities adopted speech codes aimed at wiping out racist, sexist, homophobic, and ethnic slurs. At the University of Michigan in the late 1980s, students were warned that they could be suspended or expelled for any act "verbal or physical, that stigmatizes an individual on the basis of race, ethnicity, religion, sex, sexual orientation, creed, national origin, ancestry, age, marital status, handicap, or Vietnam status." If no one else was present when the alleged hate speech occurred—if it was one person's word against another's—then the accused was presumed guilty (quoted in Sykes, 1992).

The main complaint against hate speech codes is that such regulations violate the free speech clause of the First Amendment. On these grounds some courts have decided that hate speech codes are unconstitutional. The courts have used the same reasoning to overrule the attempts of feminists to prohibit pornography.

But those who see hate speech and pornography as acts that put victimized groups at risk have mounted strong counterarguments. Their argument against hate speech is that it promotes and perpetuates social inequality. MacKinnon (1993, p. 99) argues: "Group based enmity, ill will, intolerance, and prejudice are the attitudinal engines of the exclusion, denigration, and subordination that make up and propel social inequality; that without bigotry, social systems of enforced separation, ghettoization, and apartheid would be unnecessary, impossible, and unthinkable; that stereotyping and stigmatization of historically disadvantaged groups through group hate propaganda shape their social image and reputation, which controls their access to opportunities more powerfully than their individual abilities ever do; and that it is impossible for an individual to receive equality of opportunity when surrounded by an atmosphere of group hate."

In the matter of pornography, MacKinnon simply denies that pornography can ever be construed as the expression of free speech. She maintains that pornography is a violation of women's civil rights. It defames women as a group, subordinates them, and perpetuates their condition of inequality. Pornography, she argues, promotes bigotry and contempt, as well as fosters acts of aggression, thereby harming women's opportunities for equality of rights in employment, education, access to and use of public accommodations, and acquisition of real property.

As MacKinnon sees the matter, hate speech and pornography violate the Fourteenth Amendment, which supposedly guarantees equal protection to all citizens. According to her reading of the Fourteenth Amendment, the government must protect people from demeaning and denigrating speech if they are to be and feel equal. She points out that the law of equality and the law of freedom of speech are on a collision course in this country. The law of equality, she insists, should have precedence because freedom of speech rests on the doctrine of procedural, not substantive, equality. So, when the courts defend hate speech and pornography as freedom of speech they pay no attention to what is said, the substance of the speech; they pay heed only to the act of speech itself. Therefore, in the name of free speech, the courts defend the speech acts of Nazis and the Ku Klux Klan, as well as pornographers. MacKinnon concludes that the doctrine of procedural equality benefits only the dominant groups in the society: whites, males, and gentiles. They have been given the right to defame subordinate groups, such as women, blacks, and Jews, thereby putting them at risk.

What is at issue here is the perennial conflict between the individual and the society, or as it is usually characterized today, the conflict between group rights and individual rights.[1] Those who contend that group rights have precedence over individual rights argue that in this society most people are actually treated not as individuals but as members of a group. Here, they can quote Justice Felix Frankfurter: "[A] man's job and his educational opportunities and the dignity accorded him may depend as much on the reputation of the racial and religious group to which he willy-nilly belongs, as on his own merits (quoted in Mackinnon, 1993, p. 84).

This being so, those who belong to subordinated groups in the society—blacks and women—can never have equality of opportunity so long as the group they belong to is subordinate. Hate speech and pornography perpetuate this subordination, hence the egalitarians, who support group rights, conclude that the society must collectively condemn and prohibit such conduct. An increasing number of people agree that hate speech and pornography must be prohibited by the society including many lawyers, many college administrators, many students, many academicians.[2] Many editors do, too: In an editorial on May 12, 1991, The New York Times announced that: "The real danger is the rising tide of hate." These defenders of hate speech codes see themselves as defenders of free speech—not according to its intrinsic value or its value to democratic government, but according to its contribution to the quest for equality: All have an equal right to free speech but not when it harms others or puts them at risk.

The city of St. Paul was one of several municipalities that passed a hate speech ordinance in the 1980s. Although the Supreme Court found it to be unconstitutional in June 1992, the list of organizations that appeared before the court to *defend* that hate speech ordinance is impressive. They included the Asian-American Legal Defense Fund, the NAACP, the Anti-Defamation League of B'nai B'rith, People for the American Way, the Young Women's Christian Association of the USA, the Center for Constitutional Rights, the Center for Democratic Renewal, the National Council of Black

---

[1] In 1993, the Individual Rights Foundation entered the field to represent students and faculty members whose first Amendment rights were threatened by speech codes, sexual harassment codes, and affirmative action programs.

[2] Witness the title of a recent book by Stanley Fish (1994): *There's No Such Thing as Free Speech . . . and it's a Good Thing Too.*

Lawyers, the National Council of La Raza, the International Union, United Automobile, Aerospace and Agricultural Implement Workers of America (UAW), the National Organization of Black Law Enforcement Executives, the National Lawyers Guild, the United Church of Christ Commission for Racial Justice, the National Institute Against Prejudice and Violence, the Greater Boston Civil Rights Coalition, the National Coalition of Black Lesbians and Gays, and the National Black Women's Health Network.

In July 1993 the Equal Employment Opportunity Commission prepared new rules that defined "workplace harassment" to prohibit speech (or "verbal conduct") that "denigrates or shows hostility or aversion toward an individual because of his/her race, color, religion, gender, national origin, age, or disability, or that of his/her relatives, friends or associates."

The most active promotion of hate speech codes has taken place on college campuses. By 1992, more than 300 institutions of higher learning had hate speech codes or punished such speech as a part of their overall rules of conduct (Hentoff, 1992). At present, according to *The Defender,* the publication of the Individual Rights Foundation, more than 384 public institutions of higher learning have enacted speech codes, and "the number of private colleges with speech codes may be even greater" (May, 1994). A recent survey by *The Chronicle of Higher Education* revealed that 60% of college students think that some form of speech code is necessary. They believe that speech must be limited if racism, sexism, and homophobia are to be extirpated in and out of the classroom. In addition, many cite an educational reason for speech codes: Hate speech creates a hostile environment that impairs the education of women, blacks, and homosexuals, therefore it must be prohibited if there is ever to be equality of educational opportunity. Moreover, Title VI of the Civil Rights Act guarantees equal access to the benefits of an education. Most of the defenders of speech codes embrace punishment, and, if necessary, banishment of students or professors guilty of such actions. Only by eliminating speech that makes minorities, women, and gays feel at risk, they say, will it be possible to have true equality on campus.

THE 1991 CIVIL RIGHTS ACT

The most sweeping embodiment of the new egalitarianism that seeks to avert risks to victimized groups is the Civil Rights Act of 1991, which applied to women as well as racial minorities. This act strengthened affirmative action, incorporated disparate impact as

the criterion for civil rights discrimination, and included the presumption that employers are guilty until proven innocent if their
work force does not match the racial hue of potential employees.

The avowed purpose of this Civil Rights Act was to circumvent a series of Supreme Court decisions that had weakened affirmative action. In 1989, in *Ward's Cove Packing Company v. Antonio*, the
Court had shifted the burden of proof of job discrimination to employees, declaring that employers should be presumed innocent until
employees who claimed discrimination could show that a job standard was unfair. In a second case that same year, *Richmond v. J. A.
Cruson Company*, the Court had sanctioned reverse discrimination
suits, declaring that even though a company had signed a consent
decree agreeing to racially balance its work force, this could not bind
the employer's relations with people who were not involved in the
agreement. In other words, a company could not provide preferential
treatment to minorities if that meant damaging the interests of
whites—so, if a white person was the victim of an affirmative action
program, he had the right to sue.

The 1991 Civil Rights Act not only circumvented these
Supreme Court decisions, it also provided for financial restitution as
well as punitive damages in cases of job discrimination. Enforcement
of the Civil Rights Act has fallen on the shoulders of the various
offices of the executive branch of the Federal Government. The
Department of Education monitors the affirmative action programs
of colleges and universities with regard to hiring staff and faculty
and in student admissions. Thus, the DOE tried to sanction
Occidental College for its failure to enforce its sexual harassment
code and threatened to force it to punish fraternity members. Banks
are monitored by the Federal Reserve, which has prevented them
from refusing to provide loans to people on the basis of credit rating,
assets, job history, or other predictors of repayment, if these criteria
have a disparate impact on minorities.

One of the critical players in enforcing the Civil Rights Act is
the Equal Employment Opportunity Commission (EEOC). Between
1989 and 1993 the total number of discrimination cases newly filed
with the EEOC climbed 57%, to 88,000. The EEOC now considers as
unfair any test a firm uses that results in score averages that differ
between races. This has induced many companies to practice race
norming in tabulating test results. The EEOC has also ruled that a
requirement that applicants who have served in the armed forces
must have an honorable discharge is not a valid prerequisite. Such a
requirement has a disparate impact because blacks receive twice as
many dishonorable discharges as whites. Likewise with arrest
records: The Commission has ruled that arrest records cannot be

used to disqualify applicants because this, too, has a disparate impact on blacks.

The Labor Department is also active in enforcing the Civil Rights Act. It will not approve contracts with companies that do not practice affirmative action. The Department requires contractors to file detailed racial breakdowns of their employees, and the Office of Federal Contract Compliance Program (OFCCP) sends some of its 685 inspectors to check if there are not enough non-white workers. In 1991 the Labor Department ordered the Liberty National Bank and Trust Company of Louisville, Kentucky, to offer jobs to 18 black people it had turned down two years earlier and to pay them the amount of money they would have earned if they had taken the jobs in 1989 (minus whatever money they earned in the meantime if they had taken other jobs).

Since passage of the 1991 Civil Rights Act, the Federal Courts have also strengthened affirmation action. A U.S. District Court ordered Northern Shore Towers, a New York apartment house, to pay $245,000 to four black people who claimed they were discouraged from trying to live there because the company ads featured only white people. And the U.S. Court of Appeals for the Second Circuit ruled that the *New York Times* could be sued because it accepted real estate ads that did not depict enough non-whites. In 1991 the U.S. Court of appeals for the Third Circuit ordered the town of Harrison, New Jersey, to junk its residency requirement for hiring public employees. Such a requirement had a disparate impact on blacks because only 1% of the population of Harrison is black. The Court declared that the town must hire blacks in equal proportion to their proportion in the five surrounding counties.

THE SPECIAL CASE OF HOMOSEXUALS

So far I have argued that groups who have felt victimized in the society have been able to use computer-generated statistics to corroborate their oppressed condition and thereby secure some relief through legislation, executive orders, and court decisions. This argument is bolstered by the special case of homosexuals, who lack strong statistical data to corroborate victimization and, as a result, have been much less successful in combating discrimination.

Of all the at-risk groups in the society, we have the least amount of statistical data about homosexuals. There is not even solid statistical evidence for how many homosexuals there are in the United States. The 1950 study conducted by Alfred Kinsey found that 37% of the male sample had at least one homosexual experience.

Kinsey pointed out that people array themselves along a continuum, ranging from exclusive heterosexuality to exclusive homosexuality; so he suggested that at least 10% of the population could be classified as homosexual. But critics have questioned the validity of this figure because many in his sample were prison inmates, a group more likely to engage in homosexual activity.

In 1988, a survey by the National Opinion Research Center (NORC) found that 98.5% of sexually active adults had been exclusively heterosexual during the last year. In 1993, Louis Harris and Associates reported that a survey they conducted in 1988 indicated that 4.4% of American men and 3.6% of women had sex with a same-sex partner in the five years prior to the survey. And in 1993, The Battelle Memorial Institute of Human Affairs Research Center in Seattle reported a survey that 2.3% of men aged 20 to 39 said they had sex with a man some time in the previous 10 years (The New York Times, 1993; see also Laumann, Gagnon, Michael, & Michaels, 1994).

Most Americans favor the small percentage figures that homosexuals comprise less than 5% of the population. This, some homosexuals explain, allows them to deny that there are many homosexuals around for them to think about. Tellingly, a 1985 Los Angeles Times survey showed that 50% of Americans believe that they are not personally acquainted with even one gay person (Los Angeles Times, 1985)

Not only is there no solid statistical data on the number of homosexuals in the society, there are no reliable statistics on the victimization of homosexuals. This is due to the fact that many gay victims are understandably reluctant to admit to authorities the reason why they were attacked. One estimate claims that 80% of all attacks on gays go unreported (Kirk & Madsen, 1989). But a second reason for the absence of statistics documenting how much at risk homosexuals are is the fact that legislators and law enforcement agencies have deliberately discouraged the collection of such statistics for fear that doing so will "encourage homosexuality." In 1987, for example, one-third of the House Judiciary Committee voted to *remove* sexual orientation from a bill mandating the Justice Department to collect national statistics concerning hate crimes based on race, religion, sexual orientation, and ethnicity. Of note is the fact that the final report of the Justice Department did conclude that "homosexuals are probably the most frequent victims of hate motivated violence in America."

This absence of statistics that document victimization has meant that homosexuals remain "fair game," subject to public displays of hostility never vented against blacks or women. Comedians and television sitcoms mock them, TV commercials deride them, callers to talk shows vilify them, and clergymen condemn them.

"Your are not gay, you are miserable. . . . You are not gay, you are polluted and filthy. . . . You are not gay, you are snared in a world of lust. . . . You will not be gay in hell, but tormented far worse than in life." And across the land, on city streets, and on college campuses, homosexuals are physically attacked.

Without strong statistical data to demonstrate that homosexuals as a group are at risk, most people facilely dismiss the anecdotal evidence about victimization. However, homosexuals are at risk; they have been deprived of rights enjoyed by other Americans.

- Twenty-five states, plus the District of Columbia, outlaw sodomy.
- Public intolerance impedes homosexuals' freedom of speech. *The Los Angeles Times* 1985 Survey found that nearly one-third of Americans said they would not allow an "admitted homosexual . . . to make a speech in their community"; moreover, about 40% of the public would not permit a book "in favor of homosexuality to become available in public libraries, nor would they allow a homosexual to teach in a college or university."
- TV and radio stations will not, as a rule, permit gay organizations to announce upcoming local events or meetings, thereby contributing to an information blackout that impedes freedom of assembly by gays.
- Public intolerance limits the rights of gays regarding work, housing, and public accommodations.
- Gay couples cannot legally marry (nor enjoy property rights therefrom), and in many communities they cannot parent natural or adopted children.

The deadly spread of AIDS in the 1980s did provide frightening statistics that showed homosexuals to be an at-risk group. Only 6% of the AIDS victims contracted the disease through heterosexual contacts. The statistics did generate sympathy and concern for gays—evident in the amount of money spent by the federal government in research on AIDS in recent years (more than has been spent on cancer research).

Yet, at the same time that the statistics on AIDS established homosexuals as a victimized minority legitimately deserving of America's protection and care, the same statistics generated increased hostility toward homosexuals. *The Los Angeles Times'* 1985 survey found that more than one in four citizens agreed that AIDS is God's chosen punishment for gays, and nearly as many thought that AIDS victims got just what they deserved.

The AIDS epidemic did prompt many homosexuals to organize locally and nationally to try to avert risks to their health, safety, and well being. In recent years the following national organizations have emerged: The National Gay and Lesbian Task Force, the Fund for Human Dignity, the Human Rights Campaign Fund, the National Gay Rights Advocates, the Lambda Legal Defense and Education Fund, the National Coalition of Black Lesbians and Gays, the Gay Men's Health Crisis, and the AIDS Action Council.

As advocates of gay rights these organizations have helped to secure some protection for homosexuals. In 1978, for example, the Civil Service Commission ruled that homosexuals may be permitted to serve as federal employees. By 1987, a dozen states, and a number of counties and municipalities, had made provisions to allow homosexuals to hold government jobs. And two states, three counties, and 28 cities made it illegal to discriminate against gays in employment and in the private sector. In 1986, New York City passed an ordinance banning discrimination against homosexuals in jobs, housing, and public accommodations. Universities and colleges have been the most responsive sector to the demands of gays. Speech codes and other rules protect them from harassment. A number of institutions of higher education now provide medical and pension benefits for homosexual partners.

Yet, these protections extend only to a small number of homosexuals in the United States. There has been no widespread national support for gay rights. In some cases there has been a backlash. In a Colorado referendum in 1990, voters defeated a Gay Rights Bill. In 1992, Oregon citizens voted on Measure Nine, which mandated that the state government officially recognize homosexuality as "abnormal, wrong, unnatural, and perverse." Voters rejected Measure Nine by a margin of 12%. But since then 23 local communities in Oregon have passed anti-gay rights initiatives. Neither have the courts done much to protect homosexuals from risk. Some courts have granted first amendment protection for such activities as public acknowledgment of one's homosexuality and advocacy of gay rights, but the Supreme Court has refused to extend broad first amendment protection to homosexuals. In *Bowers v. Hardwick* (1986) the Court refused to construe the right of privacy to protect consensual homosexual activity by adults in their own home.

Emblematic of the present status of homosexuals in America is the outcome of President Clinton's efforts to protect gays in the military. The outcome was to permit gays in the armed services so long as they remained silent about their sexual orientation, coupled with the denigrating military policy of: "Don't ask, don't pursue."

Clearly, without sufficient statistical data, homosexuals have not been able to avert the risk of victimization.

THE NEW DEMOCRACY

The efforts of minority groups to avert victimization ultimately confronted the question of democracy itself. Traditionally, Americans have subscribed to the notion that democracy is simply majority rule. But such a conception entails the consequence that the socially and politically powerless will lose out. This became clear to blacks, who, after the passage of the Voting Rights Act of 1965, discovered that although they could vote and even run for office, they could not win. The black minority was permanently excluded from meaningful political participation simply because, according to majority rule, 51% can decide 100% of the election.

It is true that in some circumstances the make-up of the majorities shifts, allowing different groups to have their interests represented. But it does not work that way for racial minorities: Racism insures that the white majority will be permanent, and blacks will be excluded forever from the governing coalition.

In 1982, Congress amended the Voting Rights Act to give blacks a realistic opportunity to elect candidates of their choice by redistricting in order to create majority-black districts. Although this gerrymandering did increase the number of black representatives in federal, state, and local governments, they were never a majority in these legislative bodies. Consequently, even though they were now members of legislative bodies, under the doctrine of majority rule black people still found themselves politically powerless and unable to have their interests satisfied.

To overcome this obstacle to authentic representation of black interests, Lani Guinier, a law professor at the University of Pennsylvania, has proposed setting aside the majority-rule notion of democracy in favor of what she calls "taking turns." Through the procedures of proportional representation, cumulative voting, and super-majority voting, different groups would be better able to participate in democratic politics (Guinier, 1994, pp. 14-17).

With proportional representation (which does exist in a number of European countries), the winner-takes-all rule would be put aside in elections; instead, the number of representatives each party or group wins would be based on the proportion of votes it received. With cumulative voting each citizen has multiple votes, and they may distribute their votes in any combination of their choice. This would give everyone an equal chance to influence election outcomes.

By combining proportional representation with the procedure of cumulative voting, blacks, Guinier argues, would be able to secure meaningful representation, without gerrymandering. In her scheme voters would be organized by interests rather than geographically. Geographic organization is always arbitrary, she points out, whereas organization according to interests better insures meaningful participation. Legislatures would be organized by interests. Vegetarians would elect vegetarians, anti-abortionists would elect anti-abortionists, with the result being legislators who would represent unanimous, not divided constituencies.

In enacting legislation, Guinier suggests the use of supermajority voting, which would require something more than a simple majority. This would empower any numerically small but cohesive group of legislators, enabling them to veto impending legislation.

Guinier presents a new conception of democracy (although, ironically, a conception not unlike that proposed by John Calhoun in his pre-Civil War attempts to empower southern voters). In place of the notion that programs with the most popular support are the programs that ought to be enacted into law, she proposes that interest groups should take turns; that is, groups whose ideas or programs are opposed by the majority should have the opportunity to enact their programs. However, although it is true that this kind of democracy would increase participation in the political process, it could destabilize the society by filling legislatures with single-issue representatives.

When the Clinton administration nominated her to be Assistant Attorney General in charge of Civil Rights, Guinier was derided by critics as "the quota queen," an advocate of a racial spoils system. President Clinton withdrew her nomination. Yet her ideas on democracy are now taken seriously. In an article on April 3, 1994, about a federal case that challenges redistricting in North Carolina, The New York Times saw her scheme as an acceptable alternative to bizarre gerrymandering.[3]

Guinier's ideas on democracy, like those of MacKinnon on the first amendment, are a part of the new egalitarian ideology that is gaining adherents in America. This ideology maintains that no group should be excluded, be put at risk, or ever lose more than anyone else. These are inherent characteristics of what I have called a *risk-aversive society*—a society more conscious of risks than ever before and more determined to avert them, whether these be risks to the environment, risks to the health and safety of everyone, or risks to the well being of minority groups.

---

[3]The article bears the heading, "Guinier ideas, once seen as odd, now get serious study."

I have tried to trace the origins of this risk-aversive society to the electronic computer. By compiling information about activities in the society and processing it into mathematical data presented in tables, charts, and graphs, computers have made us more conscious than ever before of the risks we confront. Some of these risks—health, safety, and environmental—affect all of us; others are risks that confront minority groups, like blacks, women, and homosexuals. In all cases, however, this heightened awareness of risk has provoked an outcry from those who subscribe to the ideology of egalitarianism: They complain that people are not getting the equal protection to which they are entitled. This failure to protect all equally is blamed on the system—the government, business, industry, and traditional institutions.

Over the last 25 years we have witnessed far-reaching actions taken to manage risk by reconstructing the society through rules, regulations, and controls. But these efforts at risk management have raised the hackles of those who subscribe to the ideology of individualism. They resent and oppose all attempts to control and stifle liberty and freedom. Moreover, when the hapless efforts of the experts—legislators, judges, and regulatory agencies—to avert risks have actually created social disharmony, then those who adhered to the ideology of hierarchy suffered a deep loss of confidence in the wisdom and competence of traditional authorities.

So, although the society has improved—everyone is more environmentally conscious, more health and safety minded, and more aware of racism, sexism, and elitism than ever before—the society is nevertheless more destabilized: People of all ideological persuasions are more suspicious and hostile toward the government, toward business and industry, and toward other groups. As society improves the strain becomes harder to bear.

PART THREE

A RISK-AVERSIVE ECONOMIC WORLD

8

THE FOURTH STAGE OF ENTREPRENEURIAL ACTIVITY

In *The Wealth of Nations*, published in 1776, Adam Smith identified those arrangements that create wealth. First and foremost are "the self-interested actions of competing individuals [entrepreneurs] who—unbeknownst to the agents themselves—coordinate to produce surplus or wealth that can benefit not only the individuals who originally generate it, but their communities as well." As Smith saw it, the entrepreneur is the creator of wealth. The entrepreneur is an innovator, a risk taker, who tries to eliminate waste and inefficiency in the utilization of time, labor, capital, and resources in his economic enterprises. To this end, the entrepreneur forms new business ventures; introduces new products; initiates new technologies of production, distribution or merchandising; alters prices to forestall competitors; strikes out in new territory to identify new markets; identifies new sources of finance; and changes internal patterns of organization.

There have been four different periods since the middle ages wherein we find an upsurge of entrepreneurial activity, resulting in dramatic increases in wealth. Each of these periods is directly connected to technological developments that helped to uncover inadequacies in the existing economic arrangements and/or provided new ways to reconstruct those arrangements.

It all began when Gutenberg invented the moveable type printing press in the 15th century. This led to the so-called commercial revolution, when, for the first time, ocean-going freighters were built that could carry payloads across long distances. The commercial revolution was made possible by the fact that the printing press could reproduce innumerable copies of maps and navigation charts, as well as plans and designs for naval instruments and vessels, all of which could be scattered everywhere to the would-be entrepreneurs of Europe (Perkinson, 1995).

The second wave of entrepreneurial activity began in the middle of the 18th century. During this so-called industrial revolution, the factory system of production gradually became dominant in most western nations. Factory production was made possible by two technological developments. First, steam engines and steam-powered machinery mechanized production and greatly increased the quantity of goods produced. Second, the substitution of iron and steel for wood in fabricating machinery and other parts changed the size, longevity, precision, and mechanical complexity of a wide variety of products— from sewing machines to ships.

The third stage of entrepreneurial activity began in the 1870s. This is what James Beniger (1986) has called the *control revolution*. During this period, large corporations rose as a result of using new technologies—primarily electric—to impose both quantitative and qualitative controls on their economic enterprises. These technologies included the telegraph, the telephone, radio, teletype, as well as the assembly line, pneumatic devices, electric magnets, photoelectric cells, electric calculators, and typewriters.

The fourth period of surge in entrepreneurship was ushered in by the electronic computer, which first became widely used in business in the late 1970s. The computer was originally introduced simply to improve existing operations in office management, retailing, manufacturing, and finance. Everyone recognized that the computer could perform tasks much more rapidly than human beings, tasks like operating machine tools, designing parts, entering data on forms, filing forms, processing payrolls, cashing checks, totaling orders, analyzing stocks, and maintaining inventories. Indeed, the computer performed these operations so rapidly that they overcame the barriers of space and time. This meant that tasks that had been performed sequentially could now take place simultaneously, thus eliminating wasted time, labor, capital, and physical resources.

More importantly, in addition to the rapidity with which it performed tasks, the computer also helped to uncover waste and inefficiency in existing operations. This happened because the computer mathematized all tasks and operations. Thus, the computer converted procedures into processes; that is, activities heretofore performed by humans (procedures) were converted into abstract mathematical and algorithmic equations that could be encoded or programmed into an electronic computer that would then perform the task (a process). Once the operations of a store, firm, bank, factory, or office had been encoded in mathematical equations and displayed graphically on a computer screen or a computer printout, entrepreneurs could view them and critically appraise them in ways never possible before.

When they looked at the operations now encoded in the computer, businessmen realized that most of the activities performed in manufacturing, retailing, and offices and firms, all have to do with information—the storage, retrieval, processing, and transmission of information. Manufacturing, for example, consists of the organization and control of activities like the shaping, cutting, mixing, molding of materials and assembling them into parts—all of which involves information, as does the activities of testing, analysis, and inspection of products, not to mention the information involved in stock control, purchasing, scheduling, shaping, and so on. Office management, too, was revealed as consisting of activities concerned with information: typing (processing information), recording and filing (storing and retrieving information), mailing, telephoning, telexing, and faxing (transmitting information). In banking, too almost all that takes place—recording debits and credits, processing checks, preparing statements—are information activities.

Once they viewed all these activities as information activities, entrepreneurs were able to uncover inefficiencies and waste in the existing operations. This resulted in dramatic reorganizations in all our economic institutions. The computer, then, has enabled entrepreneurs to introduce innovations in retailing, manufacturing, office management, banking, and finance,that have not only transformed the economic landscape, but have also helped to make the United States the wealthiest nation in the history of the world.

The Gross National Product (GNP),[1] which is the conventional index used to measure wealth, is usually reported in relative percentages. Thus, we are told that the GNP grew 4.0% in the 1970s and dropped dropping to 2.2% in the 1980s. But this gives only a measure of the relative growth of wealth. The absolute figures give a better understanding of the actual increase of wealth in the United States. According to Robert Hamrin, it took 189 years for the United States to reach the first $1 trillion GNP mark, which happened in 1970. Seven years later it reached the $2 trillion; four and a half years later, it got to the $3 trillion, and only three years later, in 1985, reached the $4 trillion (Hamrin, 1988).

---

[1]in 1991, the Federal government replaced the GNP with the GDP (Gross Domestic Product) because it believed it produced a better picture of actual economic growth.

Table 8.1 shows the increase in gross national product, industry by industry, from 1965 to 1988 (Economic Report of the President, 1991, p. 298).

The fourth age of entrepreneurship ushered in by the computer promoted unprecedented economic growth, but it also generated economic risk aversion. In Chapter Nine I discuss how risk aversion spread among workers who experienced job displacement during this fourth age of entrepreneurship. And in Chapter Ten, I describe how an even deeper and more widespread economic risk aversion emerged when egalitarians declared that ever-rising job dislocations were the result of the selfish behaviors of the new entrepreneurs. This heightened risk aversion led to demands for increased government regulation of the economy, which brought the fourth age of entrepreneurship to an end.

TABLE 8.1. GROSS NATIONAL PRODUCT BY INDUSTRY, 1947-88 (BILLIONS OF DOLLARS).

Year	Gross national product	Agriculture, forestry, and fisheries	Mining	Construction	Gross Domestic Product — Manufacturing Total	Durable goods goods	Non-durable goods	Transportation and public utilities	Wholesale and and retail trade	Finance insurance and real estate	Services	Government and government enterprises	Statistical discrepancy	Rest of world
1965	705.1	24.2	14.0	34.7	198.4	118.4	80.0	62.6	115.0	98.9	74.6	78.2	-1.2	5.8
1966	772.0	25.3	14.6	37.9	217.4	130.8	86.6	67.4	124.1	106.9	82.5	88.1	2.1	5.6
1967	816.4	24.9	15.2	39.7	222.9	133.7	89.2	70.7	132.9	115.6	90.6	98.4	-.4	6.0
1968	892.7	25.7	16.2	43.5	243.6	146.1	97.5	76.4	146.8	125.1	99.1	110.5	-1.1	6.8
1969	963.9	28.6	17.1	48.7	257.1	154.2	102.9	82.6	159.2	136.3	440.5	121.0	-3.9	6.8
1970	1,015.5	29.9	18.7	51.4	252.3	145.9	106.3	88.4	168.7	145.8	120.2	134.0	-1.1	7.3
1971	1,102.7	32.2	18.8	56.5	265.7	153.8	111.9	97.1	183.7	161.4	130.2	145.9	1.8	9.3
1972	1,212.8	37.4	20.2	63.0	292.5	172.6	119.9	108.0	202.6	174.8	144.6	160.1	-1.6	11.2
1973	1,359.3	56.2	23.4	70.4	326.4	195.4	131.0	118.7	225.6	190.5	163.2	173.1	-4.3	16.2
1974	1,472.8	55.0	36.9	74.5	338.5	201.7	136.7	129.1	246.0	206.7	179.4	189.0	-1.7	19.5
1975	1,598.4	56.3	41.3	76.5	357.3	206.3	151.0	141.7	273.7	221.7	199.8	210.1	2.5	17.5
1976	1,782.8	55.7	46.0	86.2	409.3	239.7	169.7	160.4	299.7	246.1	224.9	229.7	3.6	21.1
1977	1,990.5	58.9	50.2	97.9	465.3	277.7	187.7	178.9	332.8	280.3	253.4	247.4	.0	25.4
1978	2,249.7	70.1	56.5	115.6	518.8	317.4	201.4	201.0	373.4	326.63	289.1	270.3	-1.9	30.5
1979	2,508.2	83.1	72.7	131.4	561.85	345.2	216.5	216.1	415.8	363.3	328.7	292.4	-1.0	43.8

TABLE 8.1. GROSS NATIONAL PRODUCT BY INDUSTRY, 1947-88 (BILLIONS OF DOLLARS) (CONT.).

1980	2,732.0	77.2	107.3	137.7	581.0	3251.8	229.2	240.8	438.9	400.6	374.0	322.1	4.9	47.6
1981	3,052.6	92.0	143.7	138.4	643.1	385.8	257.6	269.6	483.1	449.3	422.6	354.7	4.1	52.1
1982	3,166.0	89.6	132.1	140.9	634.6	362.5	272.1	288.4	206.5	475.1	463.6	383.9	-.1	51.2
1983	3,405.7	74.3	118.4	149.6	683.2	385.6	297.6	320.0	542.9	536.4	515.5	410.5	5.2	49.9
1984	3,772.2	92.9	119.4	171.5	771.9	451.1	320.8	354.4	613.9	572.8	580.2	442.5	5.4	47.4
1985	4,014.9	92.0	114.2	186.6	789.5	458.8	330.8	374.1	658.2	639.5	648.1	476.7	-4.8	40.7
1986	4,231.6	93.6	74.3	203.8	832.4	478.1	354.6	3943.9	682.5	696.3	717.6	503.5	-1.8	34.4
1987	4,524.3	98.3	77.0	216.9	872.1	495.4	376.6	415.9	724.8	764.9	792.7	535.9	-4.7	
1988	4,880.6	99.8	80.4	232.6	948.6	530.3	418.3	441.4	780.8	830.3	872.5	570.6	-9.6	33.3

9

THE CREATION OF A RISK-AVERSIVE WORKFORCE

Prior to the coming of the computer humans carried out most of the transactions in the economic world, carried them out as procedures, conducted more or less routinely, properly, steadily, and more or less correctly. But the computer transformed these procedures into processes, in which the transactions were conducted automatically and without error. This transformation of the workplace began in the 1960s—in stores, factories, and offices.

RETAILING

Perhaps the element of computer technology most familiar to Americans is the Universal Product Code, or "bar code" as most call it (the black lines and numbers that appear on products sold in supermarkets and most retail stores). Today, more than 95% of all food items have bar codes. Designed originally to speed up long lines and to prevent errors at checkout counters (electronic scanners read the bar code faster and more accurately than the human eye can read the numbers), the bar code has dramatically revolutionized retail merchandising. The electronic scanner not only registers the price of the item on the cash register, it also abstracts information from the bar code, which is then transmitted to a store or central computer where it can be processed and analyzed in ways never possible before.

111

Now managers can easily trace goods without extra paper work or time-consuming data processing. They can monitor and control inventory, compare brands, update prices, measure the shelf life of goods, and evaluate the displays and placement of goods in a store. Merchandise managers can use direct product profitability programs to determine just how much they make on each product. Then, by interrelating items when customers buy several different products, merchants can infer patterns of purchasing that help them formulate merchandising plans—plans that avert some of the economic risks they had before absorbed.

The information retail stores now possess has reorganized the retail business, bringing in its wake what Alvin Toffler calls a "powershift" (1990, pp. 95-106). Before the introduction of the computer, major food processors and manufacturers sent out their sales representatives to push their products on supermarkets and retail stores. Because the manufacturers and food processors controlled the advertising and the distribution of their own products, they claimed to know how, where, when, and to whom their products would sell. Hence the sales representative could usually tell the store how much and what sizes to buy, how to display the products, when they would be delivered, and sometimes what the price would be.

But now, armed with information generated by their own computers, each retail store knows much more about the actual merchandising of products than the producers could ever know. So, instead of the manufacturers telling the store how much to take, the store makes the manufacturers pay what is known as "push money" for shelf space.

Not only the manufacturers, but others in the chain of retailing, are affected by this new-found, computer-based, power of the retail stores: wholesalers, warehouses, and transport firms now must comply with the schedules, standards, and needs that the retail stores impose on them.

The computer has done more than allow retail merchants to formulate more efficient and more effective merchandising plans. By converting procedures into processes the computer has laid out a clear picture of all the transactions that take place in a retail firm—or in any firm, for that matter: the key trends and events, industry market figures, financial information, and industry statistics. Moreover, by using the computer to perform many of the transactions—ordering, distribution, inventory control, payables, and receivables, for example—employers can increase efficiency and lower risks. Employers further reduce costs by converting documents and other information into data that can be stored, distributed, accessed, and processed by computers and special program workstations.

By making retail merchandising more efficient, the electronic computer has created more wealth. As Table 8.1 showed, the contributions of wholesale and retail trade to the GNP rose about five-fold between 1970 and 1988 from $168.7 billion to $780.8 billion. And, as always, it is those companies that have been the most innovative in using new technology who have reaped the most profits. Wal-Mart, for example, bypasses independent manufacturer's representatives to deal directly with its suppliers and imposes on the manufacturers rigid requirements for accuracy in the numbers, sizes, and models of products, as well as delivery schedules. By installing electronic networks that hook up the retail checkout counter to the manufacturer, they have compressed the time between order and delivery from weeks to days, thus enabling stores to make huge cuts in inventory. Wal-Mart expanded from 38 stores with annual sales of $.03 billion in 1970 to 1,528 stores with annual sales of $2.8 billion in 1990. As Vance Trimble pointed out, this explosion in retailing would not have been possible "without the computer" (1991, p. 264).

COMPUTER INTEGRATED MANUFACTURING

Manufacturing provides more than a fifth of the GNP and national income. From 1970 to 1985, industrial production in the United States rose by 65%. Much of this increase came about because of the introduction of computer-integrated manufacturing (CIM).

Computers were first applied in continuous process manufacturing—oil refineries, chemical processing, food and beverages, paper and pulp—to serve as simple data collection devices that gathered data and set off alarms under critical conditions. Later, computers were used to create "open loop" systems, in which operators used data generated by computers built into the system to conduct mathematical analyses to help adjust process conditions.

More recently, process control systems have appeared that are programmed to receive information directly from instruments monitoring the process, to set control points, to perform computations, and to adjust control variables to continually approximate optimum levels of functioning. Workers operate from remote control rooms where they monitor the video terminals that display data reflecting the state of the production process.

In the second sector of manufacturing, that of discrete parts—automobiles, farm equipment, and electronics, for example—one of the earliest applications of the computer was the introduction of numerically controlled machine tools (N/C). The motions that the machine tool maker performs in the manufacture of a part are described in detail mathematically and programmed into a computer that controls the operation of the machine. With numerical control, the *procedures* of producing a machine part—formerly carried out by a machinist through sight and sound and feel—is converted into a *process* spelled out precisely in mathematical and algorithmic terms.

Numerical control resulted in improved accuracy and greater quality control. Not only was there less waste and reduced scrap, but machinists required less training time. Numerical control greatly heightened both flexibility and diversity in the manufacturing process. With numerical control, manufacturers can make a range of products on one tool. Moreover, some machines can change their tools automatically, allowing them to carry out many operations on the same piece. Because the machine can run continuously, manufacturers can now produce customized parts in small batches without risk of dead time. Customized small batch production means less inventory, hence smaller warehouse space and more flexible scheduling.

What really sparked the speed up of numerically controlled machine tools in discrete parts manufacturing was the development of computer graphics, which made computer-aided design (CAD) possible. Instead of the labor-intensive drafting board, the designer uses a computer along with a light-wand to define and illustrate in numerical form the part to be produced. The calculations used in producing the part are included in the computer program. According to Pat Choate, by using CAD engineers at Rockwell International, produced two to four times as many drawings in 1985 as they had done by hand in 1981 (Choate & Linger, 1986, p. 17).

CAD not only makes designing less laborious, it actually improves design by allowing engineers to try out many different variations—something not possible before. CAD also provides automatic detection of defects in the program for parts production before the programs are used, as well as providing accurate specifications for quality control inspection.

General Motors, which pioneered the use of CAD for the design of automobile bodies, was the first to use industrial programmable manipulators—robots—for arc welding and spray painting. The Robot Institute of America defines robots as "programmable, multifunctional, manipulators, designed to move material parts, tools, or special devices, through variable programmed motions for the performance of a variety of tasks" (Quellette, Mangold, & Cheremisinoff, 1983). By using computer assisted manufacturing, in the 1980s GM could produce 150 cars per hour with the same number of employees that used to produce 115 per hour.

The integration of computer controlled systems created what came to be called flexible manufacturing systems (FMS). Here, linkages of computer-based controls dictate what will happen at each stage of the manufacturing process. By connecting production, stock control, scheduling, material management, sales, and shipping, the computer transforms the entire factory into a single machine that creates more wealth: The computers reduce the labor input, reduce the skill input, reduce lead time in design, and delivery, and reduce unit costs of production; as well as improving product design, quality, and process control. Moreover, by increasing the continuity of the production process in discrete parts manufacturing, CIM brings this sector closer to the continuous manufacturing sector insofar as computers have maximized both continuity and controllability such that workers now serve only to monitor and control the production process.

More than this, as Robert Reich (1991) has pointed out, CIM has shifted manufacturing in the United States from high-volume production to high-value production. This has brought about a reconfiguration of the way manufacturing is organized. In place of the old hierarchical organization, manufacturing companies increasingly take the shape of enterprise webs. These webs eliminate middle management—whose role in the old hierarchical organization was simply to facilitate the passage of information up or down the hierarchy. Many of these enterprise webs are international; computers and other electronic media link groups in one nation to combine their skills with those located in other nations.

Companies now outsource and contract out operations heretofore done in the United States. New York Life has shifted its claims work to Ireland, McGraw-Hill processes its journal subscriptions there, and there, too, Traveler's Insurance writes its software in Ireland. American Airlines employs over a 1000 employees in Barbados to enter data into its computers. International telephone circuits, numbering 17,000 in 1988, carry designs, data, and images back and forth between groups working in different continents (Reich, 1991).

OFFICE TECHNOLOGY

Computers were first used in office management in the 1960s for data processing (DP)—payroll and accounting, for example, and other clerical activities that involved repetitive, high-volume transactions based on applying automatic rules, calculations and formulae. In a short time, many recognized that by taking these *procedures*, formerly performed manually by humans, and converting them into *processes* conducted electronically, the computer had transformed data into information that management could use for planning and administration—to spot trends, uncover problems, and conduct competitive analyses.

The improved computer technology of the 1970s, by eliminating much of the duplication and redundancy the database companies had been using, now permitted user access at the item level. This meant that managers could request very complex searches to answer questions such as: "Show me all the customers in zip code 20001 who have purchased $500 or more of our services," or "Find all employees in the salary range 'x to y' who have not been promoted in the last five years, indicate their departments and evaluation scores, and identify their evaluators."

Throughout the 1960s and the 1970s, only the largest businesses could afford computers and the highly trained staff needed to operate them. The invention of the microprocessor—the computer on a chip—greatly increased the use of computers in offices. Microprocessors were initially embedded into other machines—everything from microwave ovens to calculators to automobiles—but they also were used to power personal computers (PCs). By 1981 more than 2 million personal computers sat on desks in offices and homes; by 1982, there were 5.5 million. In 1983 alone, people bought about 3.5 million computers. In that year Time magazine designated the computer as "Man of the Year."

During the 1980s, the development of the personal computer made computers about as commonplace as the office copier. Personal computers, along with developments in telecommunications, brought an explosive growth in information innovation and support systems. Computers could now be located anywhere and linked to any other department or company. Computers were used for spreadsheets, word processing, desktop publishing, electronic mail, local area networking, and shared data resources. Computers transformed customer service and brought about highly coordinated just-in-time ordering from suppliers.

Once the computer eliminated the barriers of space and time, office managers could focus on eliminating work rather than automating it. Thus, in many firms more and more work is contracted out, stock and inventory record keeping are reduced by just-in-time suppliers, and lead times are reduced—all of which increases wealth by cutting costs. For example, "very quick" response firms in the fabric industry take 10 days from the time they get an order from a store to when they deliver the goods, whereas "average response" firms take 125 days. The same patterns and impacts have taken place in the logistical systems of insurance firms with regard to "lead time" and in manufacturing firms with regard to "time to market."

The Emergence of a Risk-Aversive Work Force

The computer created an abstract economic world. In manufacturing, retailing, and offices, more and more people now interact (interface?) with electronic computers, not humans. This is the essence of the fourth era of heightened entrepreneurial activity, an era that generated the greatest economic growth in the history of the world. This unprecedented entrepreneurial activity raised the GNP from $705.1 billion in 1965 to $4,880.2 billion in 1988 (see Table 8.1).

The electronic computer created new industries—space and biotechnology come immediately to mind, not to mention computer industries themselves (Apple, Microsoft, Lotus, Borland International, Texas Instruments, Compaq, Sun Microsystems)—most of which became multimillion dollar companies. The electronic computer also reconfigured established companies by revealing inadequacies in the existing practices, policies, procedures, and arrangements, and by creating new, more efficient, and more profitable ways to utilize labor, time, space, capital, and raw materials.

In addition to helping them become more efficient, the computer helped American industries become more flexible in their operations. Downsizing, outsourcing, and specialization enabled many manufacturing companies to move from high-volume to high value production. Moreover, although the workplace had become more abstract, firms became less hierarchical and less centralized. The computer created flatter, more web-like, management structures and conferred new decision-making powers on those who manned each workstation.

Most of all, the electronic computer increased productivity. The Bureau of Labor Statistics Index of manufacturing productivity reached 136.9 in 1990, compared with 96.6 in 1980. In other words, as Robert Bartley put it: "Manufacturing output per employer was gaining at a rate of more than 3.5 percent a year" (1990, p. 141).

But that was the problem.

The introduction of the computer reduced transaction costs, which brought about increased output per employee hour. But in reducing their economic risks, the owners, employers, and managers increased economic risk to their employees. The computer eliminated some jobs, downgraded others, upgraded still others, and contracted out many of those that remained. The job dislocations many employees now confronted generated a great deal of risk aversion in the American work force.

Prior to the coming of the computer, experienced, competent, employees were essential to retail and manufacturing companies—

their knowledge, expertise, and abilities kept each company going. But once computers were introduced, this employee knowledge and expertise could be programmed into the computer, which was able to perform the work as well, if not better.

By the 1980s not only were typewriters, business letters, and filing cabinets on the way out—so were secretaries, stenographers, and filing clerks: replaced by cathode ray tubes, solid state memories and data storage disks, intelligent copiers and fax machines, modems, printers, digitizers, smart switchboards, and distributed computer terminals.

In addition to eliminating jobs, the computer downgraded jobs, thereby making current employees over-qualified (and over-paid) to perform them. In retail stores, instead of clerks who tally a customer's bill and calculate the amount of change due, we now have "checkers" who scan the bar code on each item; the computer both tallies the bill and calculates how much change is due to the customer. In some transactions no money changes hands at all; the customer simply uses a computerized debit card. And in some retail stores clerks not only do not need to know how to add or subtract, they no longer need social skills, since the computer electronically greets each customer with "Hello!" and ends the transaction by telling the customer to "Have a nice day!"

Another way the computer downgraded jobs was by converting full-time jobs into part-time jobs. Once computers actually performed most of the work, human employees became interchangeable—like machine parts—and could be plugged in or out of the ongoing operations of a company without causing any disruptions. Called "flex-time," this personnel practice appealed to many employers, because they did not have to provide any benefits package to part-time workers.

Although the computer downgraded some jobs, thereby making the current employee overqualified, other jobs were upgraded, thereby making the current employee underqualified to perform them. In many offices the work formerly done by file clerks, stenographers, typists, and secretaries was now conducted on computers, while comptometer operators, bookkeepers, and accountants used spreadsheet programs to do their work on computers. Without some degree of computer literacy many office employees found themselves underqualified and out of a job.

Employees in manufacturing firms experienced the same kind of job dislocation: As computers moved into factories some jobs were eliminated, others were downgraded, and some jobs were upgraded. Shoshana Zuboff (1984) has graphically described how Computer Integrated Manufacturing (CIM) caused job dislocation in a bleach plant of a pulp mill:

Before computer monitoring and control, an operator in this part of the mill would make continual rounds, checking dials and graph charts located on the equipment, opening and shutting valves, keeping an eye on vat levels, snatching a bit of pulp from a vat to check its color, sniff it, or squeeze it between his fingers ("Is it slick? Is it sticky?") to determine its density or to judge the chemical mix.

In 1981, a central control room was constructed in the bleach plant. . . .The control reflects a new technological era for continuous-process production, one in which micro-processor-based sensors linked to computers allow remote monitoring and control of the key process variables.

[W]orkers sit on orthopedically-designed swivel chairs covered with a royal blue fabric, facing video display terminals The terminals, which display process information for the purposes of monitoring and control, are built into polished oak cabinets. Their screens glow with numbers, letters and graphics in vivid red, green and blue. (pp. 19-21)

Outsourcing is another cause of job dislocation. Once the computer produced a clear picture of all the operations of a company and the transaction costs involved, employers realized that costs could be reduced if some operations were contracted out: bookkeeping, janitorial services, and data processing, for example. Often this outsourcing went, as we have seen, to foreign countries, where labor costs were less.

Automobile manufacturing provides one of the most dramatic examples of the outsourcing of jobs. According to Robert Reich (1991), GM's Pontiac LeMans is styled and designed by German engineers, assembled in South Korea with components made in Japan, advertising and market services are provided from Britain, and workers in Ireland and Barbados perform the data processing services.

In the 1980s American corporations eliminated 300,000 manufacturing jobs. Factory jobs dropped from 23% to 18% of all employment. Hardest hit were the large Fortune 500 companies. During the 1980s, blue chip companies pared their payrolls by 3.5 million employees. Employment at GE fell by one-quarter during this period. Unemployment rose higher as massive layoffs took place in the early 1990s at GM, IBM, and GTE.

And yet . . .

In spite of the incontrovertible fact of job dislocation, the unprecedented entrepreneurial activity that the computer made possible did create many, many new jobs—18 million new jobs between 1982 and 1990 alone.

It is true that in the 1970s unemployment had risen, but this was less due to the introduction of the computer into the workplace than it was to the influx of the baby-boom generation and more women into the workforce. Unemployment rose past the 10% mark in 1982. But between 1982 and 1985, roughly 9 million new jobs were created, and the unemployment rate declined to 7%, falling below that in January 1986, and breaking through the 6% barrier in September 1987. Then, in spite of the stock market crash in October of that year, unemployment continued to decline, reaching a low of 5.1% in March 1989 (Vedder & Gallaway, 1993).

According to Richard Vedder and Lowell Gallaway, two economists who have conducted extensive research on unemployment: "In the eighties jobs were created at a pace so substantial that the growth in employment exceeded the growth in the number of job holders—an unprecedented achievement in the post World War II period. Even more unprecedented was the decline in the official unemployment rate for seven consecutive years, something that never happened before" (p. 73).

If unemployment actually declined during the 1980s, then why was there so much risk aversion among the workforce? Part of the reason was that many of those the computer had put out of work or dislocated were from the college-educated middle class. This was the first time since the depression that so many of those who were unemployed were professional workers—engineers, technicians, accountants, managers, and executives. In 1990, according to Kevin Phillips (1993), 23% of the unemployment claims in Massachusetts were being filed by workers with college educations and technical or professional backgrounds. The following year unemployment nationally rose to 6.6%, and by 1993 it had risen to 7.3%. And still more and more of the unemployed workers were people who had held white-collar jobs.

These middle-class workers, stunned by the loss of their jobs, vociferously demanded an explanation of what was going on, and more than this, they wanted guarantees of job security.

THE EGALITARIAN RESPONSE

The egalitarian ideology provided both an explanation of job dislocation and a strategy for guaranteeing job security. Egalitarians construe the economy as a zero-sum game: If someone wins, then someone else must lose. Hence, the egalitarians explain, some people are being deprived of income because this allows other people to gain more income: The entrepreneurs are reaping profits at the expense of the middle and lower classes. As the saying goes: The rich get richer, and the poor get poorer.

In truth, according to all studies, the rich did get richer during the 1980s—but so did the poor. The egalitarian complaint, however, was about relative deprivation; that is, the rich had a larger percentage of the nation's wealth than ever before in history. This was also true (Krugman, 1994). The Reagan tax reductions of the 1980s left more money in the hands of the rich, who then invested it and made more money, giving them a large share of the nation's wealth. This, some argued, promoted economic growth, which provided more jobs and, therefore, benefited all (Anderson, 1990; Bartley, 1992; Lindsey, 1990).

The egalitarian critics, however, saw the matter differently (Krugman, 1994; LeKachman, 1982; Phillips, 1990). One of the most forthright egalitarian attacks came in a 9-part series that appeared in *The Philadelphia Inquirer* in 1991, entitled, "America: What Went Wrong?" It later came out as a best-selling paperback, and the reporters who wrote it, Donald Bartlett and James Steele, received a Pulitzer Prize. Here's a partial list of their charges:

> Workers will continue to be forced to move from jobs that once might have paid $8 to $20 an hour to jobs that will pay less. Some will be consigned to part-time employment. Some will lose all or part of fringe benefits they have long taken for granted. Women and blacks will continue to move into the work force, but they will receive substandard wages, substandard pensions and substandard fringe benefits. For the first time, they will be joined by a new minority—white males—in both manufacturing and service jobs. Workers will be compelled to forego wage increases to shoulder a growing percentage of the cost of their own health care coverage entirely. The elimination of jobs that once paid middle-class wages will continue uninterrupted, due in part, to an ongoing wave of corporate restructurings and bankruptcies, the continuing disappearance of some industries and the transfer of others to foreign countries. More than a half-million men and women, including many with growing families, will be dumped into this sinking job market as the Defense Department begins to deal with budget cuts by prematurely discharging military personnel—most of whom had planned on a twenty-to-thirty year career in the armed forces. (1992, pp. 11-12)

The villains in the story told by Bartlett and Steele are the American entrepreneurs who created "an orgy of debt"—much of it "to buy and merge companies, leading to the closing of factories and the elimination of jobs"—all the while securing bloated salaries for themselves. In cahoots with the businessmen were the politicians who "wrote the rulebook" that directed the course of the American economy. Congressmen, influenced by lobbyists who served special interests, prevented "tax law changes that would be detrimental to the privileged, as well as preserving tax breaks that benefit the few at the expense of the many" (1992, pp. 18, 19, 184).

Having explained unemployment and job dislocation by construing the economy as a zero-sum game, in which the rich get (relatively) richer at the expense of the (relative) deprivation of the rest, the egalitarians came out in favor of governmental regulations and tax programs to redistribute wealth. This proposal emanated from their deep and firm conviction that the distribution of wealth in America is unfair and unjust. Furthermore, they believed that the heightened entrepreneurial activity of the 1980s was nothing more than a decade of greed, a time when the selfish pursuit of wealth had weakened and threatened the American economy—clearly evident in the S&L debacle, the stock market crash of 1987, and the insider trading scandals on Wall Street.

10

THE ATTACKS ON THE NEW ENTREPRENEURS

Computers made the fourth age of entrepreneurship possible: Computers helped create new investment strategies in the stock market, computers opened up the banking field to new entrepreneurs, and computers enabled financial entrepreneurs to create a new source of venture capital in the form of "junk bonds" that business entrepreneurs used to start new companies and buy out and restructure old ones. But these entrepreneurial adventures all seemed to end up in economic disasters: the stock market crash of 1987, the frenzy of leveraged buyouts, and the S&L debacle.

WALL STREET AND THE CRASH OF 1987

Engineers, mathematicians, and computer programmers first entered Wall Street in the 1970s. Bearing the title "Computer Application Specialists," these "Quants," as they were called, initially served security analysts, helping to eliminate some of their laborious tasks. The traders also soon began to use computers too; here to perform studies on the histories of trends of companies or compare the market behavior of a stock to the average under a variety of conditions—both types of analyses helped to narrow the field of stocks worth examining. Computers could determine not only what a stock was worth but also what other traders were planning to do about it.

123

Burnham and Company was one of the first Wall Street firms to install a computer. This was in 1962, when William Tuite set one up to do back-office accounting—bookkeeping, stock records, statements, and confirmations. By enhancing its capacity to process operations, Burnham was one of the firms that survived when the surge of trading increased in the late 1960s. After acquiring Drexel and becoming Drexel-Burnham, it became one of the first firms to put in its own in-house communication system to handle message switching and order-matching traffic.

By the mid-1980s, all investment houses had their own computer systems. By this time, too, the New York Stock Exchange (NYSE), the American Exchange (AMEX), and the over-the-counter stocks traded by the National Association of Security Dealers (NASD), had all automated their quotation networks, which enabled market makers to flash bids and offers to their opposite numbers on to computer screens where quote figures were constantly updated as the bid-and-offer bargaining heated up.

Installing computers in the exchanges solved the "paper-crunch" problem that had almost swamped them in the 1960s and 1970s. In order to handle the number of transactions during that time, the floors of the exchange had shortened their hours of operation. With computers not only were they able to catch up, they dramatically increased the volume of trading. On the NYSE alone, volume surged from 4.96 billion shares in 1975 to 11.85 billion shares in 1981. As John Phelan, the Chairman responsible for automating the NYSE pointed out: "When the 100 million share days and 150 million share days came in the latter part of 1982 and continued through 1983, for the first time people really understood that they couldn't do the volume without automation."

Much of this increased volume came from institutional investors, such as pension funds, mutual funds, and corporations, all of whom—as they were equipped with computers—could manage large volumes of stocks and bonds with efficiency and ease, trading them in blocks of 5,000 or more shares. By 1980, there were over 600 mutual funds; by the mid 1980s there were over 18,000 pension funds with $1.3 billion available for investment. The volume of trading was further increased when the computer was used to create a national market system, hooking up stock exchanges across the nation, as well as connecting the stock market in New York with the futures market in Chicago.

In addition to dramatically increasing the volume of trading, the electronic computer had earlier given rise to innovative trading strategies. In 1972, mutual funds appeared that enabled investors to avoid paying brokers to select stocks for them by simply joining a mutual fund that had a composite portfolio of stocks. During the 1980s, the Reagan administration's tax policy stimulated the growth of mutual funds by encouraging millions of Americans to pour hundreds of billions of dollars into Individual Retirement Accounts (IRAs) and Keogh plans, most of which wound up in mutual funds—tripling their assets between 1982 and September 1987.

Mutual funds are often index funds in which stocks are packaged into a tradable basket that approximately mirrors broad market indexes such as the Standard and Poor 500, the Dow, and so on. The investor then has a portfolio that does pretty much what the stock market does. Computer programs select the stocks and determine how much of each stock should be in the basket.

The integration of the stock and the futures markets led to another innovative trading strategy: portfolio insurance. Here money managers hedge or insure their portfolios of stocks by buying stock options on the futures market. A stock option is a contract that enables the holder to buy (a "call" option) or sell (a "put" option) 100 shares at a stated price at any time until the expiration of the option. Money managers could "hedge" the market risk on their stock portfolios by buying put options or selling call options on any of the stocks in their portfolios. Computer analysts worked up formulas and programs that managers could use to evaluate options quickly and efficiently. Managers buy or sell whole portfolios containing from tens to hundreds of blue chip stocks with values from tens to hundreds of millions of dollars.

For block trades, this portfolio insurance resulted in what came to be called *programmed trading*. Here, cross market trading strategy takes the form of stock index arbitrage. The index arbitrageur aims to profit on divergencies in value between a bushel of stocks traded in the stock market and a comparably sized holding of futures traded in the futures market. When the basket of stocks is worth sufficiently less than the stock index futures, the index arbitrageur (the "arb") can turn a profit by selling the futures in the Chicago Mercantile Exchange and buying the cheaper basket in New York. Conversely, if the basket fetches significantly more than the futures, the arb can profitably reverse the process by buying the futures and selling stocks.

Once again, the computer wizards worked out the formulas and developed the programs to determine automatically how much stock to buy or sell and under what circumstances to buy or sell it. Programmed trading resulted in concentrated waves of $20 million or more of buying or selling, which sent stock prices gyrating in minutes. By the mid-1980s, at least $80 billion was involved in programmed trading operations.

The computer had completely changed the operation of the stock market. Traditionally, the stock market was a marketplace for the allocation of funds to public companies: Investors paid high prices for the stocks of healthy and primary companies and low prices for the stocks of weak and failing companies. The computer transformed investing into trading. As more and more of the nation's stock ownership passed into the hands of a relatively few institutional—mutual funds, pension funds, insurance companies—price movements in the market were related to computer generated statistics rather than to individual analysis of a company and how it was doing. When those who owned the stocks cared nothing about the companies whose stocks they owned, the stock market became a casino, completely removed from the fundamental analysis of investment.

Now anyone with a computer could buy and sell stocks. In recognition of this, the Security Exchange Commission (SEC) abolished set brokers' commissions in May 1975, allowing discount entrepreneurs to enter the field who would simply buy and sell stocks for customers without providing any analysis, advice, or information. The increased number of players raised the volume of trading and created a highly volatile market.

The computer, having brought into being innovative practices and instruments that heightened the volume and volatility of the market (mutual funds, block trading, indexing, portfolio insurance, programmed trading and risk arbitrage), helped to create the greatest bull market in the history of the stock market, raising the Dow-Jones average from 777 in August 1982 to 2,700 in October 1987.

The first signs of a stock market turndown came on October 14, 1987, when rumors circulated that Congress was going to pass legislation designed to limit the deductibility of interest incurred in financing takeovers. This led to a sell-off as arbitrageurs, private traders, and especially institutions, began to sell. On Thursday and Friday, October 15 and 16, the market fell more than 100 points each day. On Monday, October 19, the stock market crashed—falling 508 points, or 22.6%, in the single worst one-day loss in history. From the close of trading Tuesday, October 13, to the close of trading Monday, October 19, the Dow-Jones Industrial Average declined by about one-third, originating a loss in the value of all outstanding United States stocks of approximately $1 trillion.

According to the SEC (Brady) report on the crash, on "Black Monday" computer programs generated more than half the sale of stocks in the Standard and Poor 500 on just between 1:10 and 1:50 P.M. alone. Most of this consisted of sell orders issued by institutions, or, more accurately, by their computers.

When stocks dropped to a mathematically predetermined level, the elaborate portfolio strategies programmed into the computers to operate on automatic pilot instantly went into action—unloosing hundreds of millions of dollars worth of stocks. Without enough buyers, the prices of stocks plummeted. As institutions dumped block after block of their securities on the market, the Chairman of the NYSE called it a "financial meltdown."

The computers had not been able to keep up with the volume of sales. According to the Brady report, on Monday, October 19, an unprecedented 396 million shares were entered into the NYSE Designated Order Turnaround System (DOT), which so overwhelmed the mechanical printer that prints DOT orders that it caused significant delays in the execution of sell orders.

Because the computer had constructed an electronic global network among the stock exchanges throughout the world, the crash in New York launched a chain reaction that reverberated through Tokyo, London, Hong Kong, and elsewhere.

JUNK BONDS AND LBOs

One of the most spectacular entrepreneurial innovations made possible by the computer was the high-yield bond market, or "junk bonds" as they came to be called. Junk bonds are bonds issued by new companies, or bonds issued by companies that have taken a downturn. As such, they have below-investment-grade credit ratings so as to be regarded as high risk. In order to be sold, they must promise a high yield—higher than investment grade bonds.

Michael Milken, who made an exhaustive study of these bonds, discovered that by all statistical and economic features the market undervalued them, so a carefully selected portfolio of high-yield bonds would be a profitable investment. Through the computer, he could keep track of these bonds, as well as maintain an up-to-date analysis of their performance. In addition, the computer allowed these bonds to be securitized—packaged into large blocks so that they could be traded in the secondary market, just like home mortgages.

When he arrived in the bond trading department of Drexel-Burnham in 1979, Milken set up an online computer trading system that allowed traders to determine their exposure and their risk, as well as how much capital they needed to finance a particular trading operation. Once again, the computer made such entrepreneurship possible. As Milken put it: "Walton used retailing technology to create value; Drexel used financial technology to create value . . . by enabling entrepreneurs to raise money far more efficiently than they could have done without us" (cited in *Reason*, 1993, p. 35).

The gospel Milken preached was that for companies junk debt was an effective source of funding, and for investors it offered a high return. Financial institutions were willing to invest in junk bonds because of the attractive rate of return. Other investment houses, following the lead of Drexel-Burnham, greatly increased the underwriting of junk bonds between 1982 and 1986. By 1986, junk bonds constituted nearly one-fifth of total corporate bonds outstanding, a rise from a mere 4% just seven years earlier (the product mainly of new issue flotations). By 1987, Standard and Poor reported that more than half the firms it rated fell into the junk bond category. Junk bond funding replaced bank loans, especially for the new risky firms, as well as for rapid growth in established firms.

One of the principle uses of junk bonds was to finance takeovers or "leveraged buyouts" (LBOs) of established companies. This meant that the buyers, often called "hostile raiders," mortgaged the company, putting it into a high level of debt. During the 1980s, the names of raiders—T. Boone Pickens, Ronald Perelman, Carl Ichan, Marvin Davis, Irwin Jacobs—became familiar to readers of business news, as they sought to take over such large companies as Revlon, Phillips Petroleum, Unocal, TWA, Disney, Crown Zellerback, National Can, and Union Carbide. During the 1980s the number of mergers more than doubled, going from 1,565 in 1980 to 3,487 in 1988 (Adams &Brock, 1989).

The leveraged buyout movement took place in retail as well as manufacturing firms. These included R.H. Macy, who operated 251 stores; Federated Department Stores, who operated 140 stores, including Bloomingdale's and Abraham and Strauss; Revco (a 1,141 unit drug store chain); Ames Department Stores; Hills Department Stores; and Southbend, the owner of 7-Eleven stores.

The "raiders" cast themselves as entrepreneurs out to save American industry by unseating those corporate managers who were not serving the best interests of the corporations, nor of the corporations' stockholders. By placing the company into debt, the raiders claimed to be inducing management to meet or exceed performance standards—otherwise the company would be lost to the bond holders. Moreover, because interest payment on bonds is tax deductible, whereas stock dividends are not, debt is less expensive to the company, the raiders explained.

Not unexpectedly, some of the takeovers or leveraged buyouts (LBOs) were made by the management itself, who were in a position to realize what a company was really worth. In these management buyouts (MBOs), the management of a company would convert the company's equity into debt by issuing junk bonds to obtain the funds to buy out the company they worked for, or to buy other companies.

By buying out stockholders—at a considerable profit for the stockholders—the public company became a private one. Although the new owners remained deep in debt, the interest payments on debts were tax deductible. The Federal Government, however, did not lose money because it gained millions in tax revenue from the transactions involved in these takeovers—from 1980 to 1988 mergers and acquisitions comprised a value of almost $1.1 billion. Moreover, the new owners not only profited from the tax deductions, they also made money by downsizing or liquidating the company—selling off parts of it for more than what they had paid to take it over. Finally, the investment houses also turned over a handsome profit. At one point, Michael Milken of Drexel-Burnham earned $550 million in one year.

These leveraged buyouts drove the stock market up dramatically, because those taking over the company had to buy up the stock by paying higher than market price. Not only did investors profit, but risk arbitrageurs entered the activity when they anticipated a takeover or a buyout—quietly buying stocks in anticipation of the higher price. Historically, arbitrageurs had traded to take advantage of discrepancies in different markets, such as London and New York. But the coming of the computer, as we saw earlier, brought about index arbitrage; it also brought about risk arbitrage, in which arbs—the most famous were Ivan Boesky, T. Boone Pickens, and Carl Ichan—began trying to take advantage of mergers and takeovers, heavily buying stocks that were subject to anticipated takeover bids. Sometimes these arbs completed the takeover themselves, or threatened to do so, in return for "greenmail"—a legal blackmail.

Not everyone profited from the leveraged buyouts, however. Often the takeover went from buyout to bankruptcy. And on the way to bankruptcy, and after, the new owners downsized companies, closed plants and stores, fired workers or laid them off, demanded salary cuts or fringe benefit "give-backs," and, in some cases, cancelled expected pensions.

In spite of the bankruptcies they caused—not to mention downsizings, sell-offs, and cutbacks—the raiders insisted that what they were doing was good for American business. They found support from George Gilder (1984), who reminded everyone that the entrepreneur is a risk-taker: That's how he creates wealth. Indeed, just as scientific knowledge grows because scientists come up with risky theories, economic growth, comes about through entrepreneurial risk. Every entrepreneurial venture embodies and tests an hypothesis about products or markets. In science, when an hypothesis is falsified, this generates new knowledge and leads to the creation of a new, better hypothesis. In economic progress, bankruptcy plays the same role that falsification plays in the progress of ideas. Thus, bankruptcy can serve as an index of growth: Large setbacks are a potent of large gains, and stability is a precursor of failure.

But the egalitarians would not buy it. They insisted that the deep indebtedness of so many companies—an indebtedness that often led to bankruptcy—was a sign not of progress but of economic decay. And at the root of this decay was the ready availability of credit provided by junk bonds. Abetted by journalists like James Stewart, a reporter for the *Wall Street Journal*, who wrote the best selling *Den of Thieves* (1991), the opponents of junk bonds were able to convince the public that these bonds were a scam, peddled by crooks.

In 1986, Dennis Levine, a broker at Merrill-Lynch, was indicted for illegal trading in 54 different companies. Levine fingered Ivan Boesky, the biggest arb on the street, who was tried and convicted of insider trading. Boesky squealed on Martin Siegal, an investment banker whom Boesky had bribed with a suitcase full of cash. Boesky also blew the whistle on Michael Milken, the father of junk bonds.

Using the Racketeer Influence and Corrupt Organizational Act (RICO), Richard Giuliani, United States Attorney, indicted Milken on 98 counts. The court found him guilty of only six felonies, all of them technical violations. Levine got two years in prison, Boesky spent three years in jail, Siegal got two months, and Milken received a 10-year sentence. In sentencing Milken, Judge Kimba Wood declared: "Crimes that are hard to detect warrant greater punishment in order to be effective in deterring others from committing them" (quoted in Stewart, 1991, p. 443).

Yet, in spite of the widespread hostility toward junk bonds, they had provided a handsome return to investors: From 1981 to 1991, the junk bond market averaged returns of 14.1%, outperforming both U.S. Treasury bonds and the Dow Jones industrial average.

Furthermore, junk bonds had actually fueled the productivity of the 1980s. The proceeds from high-yield financing (junk bonds) had gone primarily to industries that had previously had limited access to capital markets controlled by conservative commercial banks. As Glenn Yago put it: "In the pharmaceuticals, chemical processing, computers, semiconductors, instruments and electronic industries, where research and development are big, junk bonds helped create and popularize innovative products and services. Motion pictures, cable television, broadcasting, health care, social services, and communications, are other sectors that have emerged as central to economic growth over the last decade and have utilized this new market effectively to grow and develop trade surpluses during an era of expanding trade deficits" (1991, p. 10).

By providing these new small and medium-sized companies with capital—capital that the commercial banks had refused to extend to them—junk bonds enabled them to raise $365 billion in debt and equity. Moreover, while the Fortune 500 companies were sending workers to the unemployment lines, these noninvestment-grade companies were creating jobs. Large firms—defined as those with annual sales over $600 million—reduced employment by 29%: from 16 million employed in 1979 to 11.5 million in 1993. During this period employment in small and medium firms grew by 28%: from 83 million to 106 million (Wolf, 1994).

Junk bonds not only created the new growth companies of the 1980s, but, as we discussed earlier, they also financed the leveraged buyouts that led to the restructuring and refocusing of established companies. Junk bonds, therefore, threatened both bankers and the managers of established companies—depriving the former of loans they might have made and threatening the latter with the loss of their jobs. This led some commentators, like Robert Bartley, to imply that most of the animus against junk bonds came from the antagonism of the old capital toward new capital—an antagonism against the new entrepreneurial actions that the computer had made possible (1992).

Bartley may have been right about this, but he did not explain why the animus extended throughout the society. As I see it the opposition was ideological and emanated from egalitarianism. It was an ideology that had gained adherents by blaming unemployment and job dislocation on junk bonds.

THE NEW BANKERS AND THE SAVING AND LOAN DEBACLE

During the fourth period of entrepreneurial activity many non-banks entered the field of banking. Thus, we find all sorts of institutions providing banking services: retail chains, like Sears; investment firms, like Merrill Lynch; finance companies, like GMAC; money funds, like Dreyfus; credit card firms, like American Express; insurance companies, like Prudential; and thrift institutions, like Savings Banks and Savings and Loan societies. All of them began offering checking accounts, loans, mortgages, lines of credit, securities, and cash management.

The rise of new banking institutions took place because the severe government regulations imposed on banks had put a ceiling on their interest rates, prohibited interstate operations, required substantial noninterest bearing reserves, and generally discouraged

innovations in financial products and instruments. But these regulations on banks had been in place since the 1930s when the federal
government had imposed them in order to prevent the competition
among banks that, it was thought, had caused the bank failures of
that time. So why had non-banks not entered the field earlier?

The answer, of course, is the computer.

Banking had always been a labor-intensive industry that prohibited other kinds of firms from taking on banking operations. But
the computer changed all this.

Take the Savings Banks and Savings and Loans. Prior to the
introduction of the computer, these institutions opened their ledgers
once per quarter to post the interest earned. Having no "back office,"
they had no staff to do this more frequently. But once the ledgers
were kept on a computer the banks could post interest every night.
All the accounts were now cycled through every day as it was easier
to run the entire customer list past the post, pausing when an entry
had to be made, than to hunt through the memory for just the
accounts that need updating.

In a short time, S&Ls and Savings Banks were offering interest "from day of deposit to day of withdrawal" and "daily compounding
of dividends." The computer also enabled savings institutions to offer
interest-bearing checking accounts called Negotiable Order of
Withdrawal Services (NOW accounts). Because banks were still subject to the regulations imposed on them in the 1930s—regulations that
prohibited them from offering NOW accounts or the daily compounding of interest—many customers were enticed to transfer their funds,
thereby shifting power away from banks to Savings Banks and S&Ls.

But the actions of the thrifts were merely the beginning of
the electronic revolution in banking. The computer eliminated labor-
intensive account work and facilitated the mobility of funds, thereby
making financial offices inexpensive to operate. As a result, as
Martin Mayer quipped: "Anyone who owns a computer can run a
bank" (1984, p. 59).

In the 1970s, new institutions, called money market funds,
appeared which further drained funds from the banks. With computers set to handle information exchange relating to financial assets,
all it took to get into business, Mary King pointed out, "was some
advertising to announce their interest rates, an 800 telephone number, and a few employees to handle the mail as the money poured in"
(1985, p. 78).

In 1973, there were four funds with assets of $100 billion; by
1980, the number of money market funds had increased to 85, with
over $800 billion in assets. Initially, only large depositors could
afford the substantial initial investment required by these funds. But

the computer facilitated the creation of money market mutual funds that allowed depositors to open an account with a minimum of $1,000—together with no sales charge and a market rate of return on savings, along with checking privileges, liquidity, and direct access to other types of investments. Within 10 years, these unregulated funds attracted 10% of consumer savings.

In 1977, Merrill Lynch exploited the money market mutual fund by combining it with its new Cash Management Account (CMA). It took Merrill Lynch 18 months and 75 people—a hundred man-years of computer programming time—to work out this new financial instrument. The CMA is ostensibly a brokerage account available to those with a minimum of $20,000 in cash and securities. It is a margin account, allowing customers to buy stocks with only partial payment, or to borrow against existing holdings by writing a check or using a VISA card. But the CMA customer has more than just another checkbook and another VISA card: He or she has assurance that money from his or her stock and bond instruments will not lie idle. When a stock is sold, the proceeds are invested automatically and immediately in the Money Trust, a money market mutual fund.

Within the decade, other entrepreneurial financial players purchased brokerage houses so they could offer their own versions of CMA. Prudential Insurance purchased Bache, American Express bought Shearson, and Sears acquired Dean Witter. Sears made the biggest splash because it already had considerable in-house computer sophistication from its pioneering use of electronics for inventory control and cash registers. In 1982, Sears moved into high gear in its financial network, opening offices across the country for its real estate brokerage house of Coldwell-Banker. By 1983, Sears had 130 "financial service centers" in its stores including stock brokerages, mortgage lending, real estate brokerages, and banking.

Now that computers had made regulatory barriers obsolescent, where were the banks?

Far behind. For, not only were banks hampered by regulations imposed by the Federal government in the 1930s that had imposed interest rate ceilings on banks, they were also less innovative, less technologically oriented, and far less aggressive in marketing retail services. By 1981, the banks controlled only 37% of the nation's financial assets, compared to 57% in 1946. Moreover, between 1979 and 1982, the percentage of consumer and business short-term assets held by banks in checking and savings deposits was reduced by 50%. The computer, by allowing many more players to enter the field, had placed banks at risk.

In retrospect, the most significant players to enter the world of banking were the Savings and Loan institutions (the thrifts). In the 1930s, in an attempt to subsidize housing (commercial banks at that time concentrated on business loans and neglected home mortgages), Congress passed a series of legislative acts—the Federal Reserve Home Loan Bank Act of 1932, the Home Owners Loan Bank Act of 1937, and the National Housing Act of 1934—that restructured the savings and loan industry. These acts both placed these institutions under Federal regulation and insured S&L deposits up to $5,000.

The thrifts collect savings accounts which they then invest in residential mortgages. These loans were backed almost wholly by residential properties, usually concentrated in a narrow geographic region, and uniformly carried long terms and fixed rates. When inflation drove interest rates up in the 1960s and 1970s, savings depositors began to withdraw their money to take advantage of the better rates available elsewhere. The S&Ls could not increase the rates on existing mortgages and could only raise their interest rates on mortgages slowly as they issued new mortgages. But the decline in deposits meant that S&Ls would have no money to lend.

In 1966, Congress made matters worse by trying to limit competition among thrifts by making it illegal for them to offer more than a set interest rate. As inflation continued to rise during the Nixon and Carter administrations—reaching double digits in 1979 and 1980—the Federal Reserve Bank responded by raising interest rates, leading more and more people to withdraw their savings from the S&Ls to put them into CDs and money market funds. In desperation, the thrifts turned to Washington: The computer had made deregulation necessary.

In March 1980, Congress passed and President Carter signed the Depository Institutions and Monetary Control Act, which was supplemented two years later by the Garn-St. Germaine Depository Institutions Act. These acts essentially freed the S&Ls to become, in effect, commercial banks. S&Ls were allowed to pay unlimited interest rates in competition with money market funds, as well as pursue a broader range of investments—consumer loans, commercial paper, and corporate debt. In addition, they could offer credit card services, hold money market funds, and issue NOW accounts.

But in the act of deregulating S&Ls, Congress also removed the discipline of funding risk from these banks. First of all, the 1982 Garn-St. Germain Act sanctioned direct federal infusions into bank capital through an exchange of notes with federal insurers. Such assistance could cover 70% of the losses for some failing thrifts. Perhaps more significant, the 1980 Act raised the maximum for deposit insurance from $40,000 to $100,000 per account, more than doubling taxpayer liability for sick thrifts.

Once Congress had removed the discipline of funding risk, the S&Ls in trouble were more likely to try to expand than contract. Saddled with long-term mortgage loans set at fixed rates of interest anywhere between 4% and 8%, the S&Ls had been for some time borrowing short term in order to stay in business. But now, both inflation and the Federal Reserve Board's tightened interest rates had driven the cost of short-term funds up to around 17.5%.

Still, many S&Ls decided to grow their way out of their problems. They began to borrow money at 17.5% and invest it in the hope of still higher returns. Much of it they invested in commercial real estate. Lenders on Wall Street cooperated because they knew that the U.S. government would pay the debts if an S&L failed.

And fail they did. The losses suffered by the thrift industry in 1981-82 were greater than those of the steel industry, the auto industry, and the agricultural-machinery industry combined, according to Martin Mayer. He adds that unorthodox accounting practices actually concealed even deeper losses (Mayer, 1984). In the early months of 1983, the Federal Savings and Loan Insurance Corporation (FSLC) closed down Chicago's Manning Savings and Loan, an $80 million institution that grew by $20 million in the 40 hours before the regulators moved in.

In 1986 Congress made matters worse for the thrifts by rescinding the tax breaks given in 1982 to commercial real estate investors. As a result, property values plunged. Heavily invested in real estate, the S&Ls saw the value of their holdings plunge

As the government-insured thrifts expanded deeper into debt, the Federal Home Loan Bank Board (FHLBB), which was supposed to oversee the thrifts, found itself hampered by certain congressmen who did not want specific thrifts closed down. In 1987, Speaker of the House, Jim Wright, held up the recapitalization bill for the thrift insurance fund in an attempt to dissuade the FHLBB from closing Vernon Savings and Loan in Texas. Because closing insolvent thrifts requires a federal payout, Wright's tactics hamstrung the efforts of the FHLBB to act. When finally seized by regulators, some 96% of Vernon's loans were in default.

The Lincoln thrift in California found defenders in the Senate. Here, the Keating Five—so-named because all five senators had received campaign contributions from Charles H. Keating, Jr., the head of Lincoln—intervened to prevent the regulators from seizing this insolvent and dishonestly operated S&L. Lincoln was ultimately closed in April 1989. By that time the bill for the taxpayers was estimated to be $2.5 billion.

Although Congress and certain congressmen were largely responsible for the S&L debacle—raising the insurance coverage in 1982, withdrawing the real estate tax breaks in 1986, and interfering with the monitoring of S&Ls—many expected Congress to bail out the S&Ls.

In its 1989 Financial Institutions Reform, Recovery and Employment Act (FIRREA), Congress insisted that all S&Ls divest their junk bond portfolios and desist from buying any more. Congress did this in spite of the fact that earlier that same year the General Accounting Office, Congress' financial watchdog, had reported that "so far, high yield junk bonds have been attractive for thrifts compared to many alternative investments, and high yield bond investments have not contributed to the thrift industry's current problems" (cited in Bartley, 1992, p. 262).

Indeed, between 1980 and 1990, junk bonds produced a 13.0% average annual rate of return, outperforming high grade corporate bonds, U.S. Government bonds, and common stocks. In forcing S&Ls to sell off their junk bond holdings Congress eliminated one of the few profitable investments the thrifts had made. Moreover, by divesting their junk bonds, some 150 thrifts automatically wrote down the capital they had, and overnight some became officially "insolvent" even though the bonds they had owned were still paying the same high interest rates. In consequence, those institutions had to be taken over by the Resolution Trust Corporation (RTC), who promptly, but ineptly, sold their assets.

Although only 5% of the 3,025 federally insured thrifts had owned any junk bonds, Congress's action made the bottom fall out of that market. Junk bond defaults hit a record $18.9 billion in 1991— 10.3% of all outstanding principle. The following year, however, default rates retreated to 3.4%, and in 1992, a record $40 billion of new junk bond issues were brought to the market (Rubinstein, 1994).

Congress's attempt to bail out the S&Ls did not reduce the federal deposit insurance, but instead sought to prevent the thrifts from doing risky things: Congress raised insurance premiums, made capital requirements higher, imposed more indirect taxes, increased regulations, and reduced diversification authority. All of these measures not only discouraged economic growth, but according to Lawrence White, one-time member of the Federal Home Bank Board, "had a rebound effect that has increased the public's costs of cleaning up the insolvents" (1991, p. 182)

After Congress carried out its risk-aversive actions, the regulators from the executive branch trotted out new guidelines that curtailed loans for corporate takeovers and restructuring: No loans were to be made to a company if their debt exceeded 75% of assets, or if there was a doubling of debt to a level above 50% of assets. Following this, banks stopped lending. In 1990, more loans were closed or withdrawn than initiated.

Without the capital supplied by junk bonds or by bank loans, entrepreneurship declined. The index of new business incorporations maintained by the Commerce Department fell from 125 in 1989 (against a base of 1987 = 100) to 113.3 in September 1991.

THE END OF AN ERA

The fourth era of entrepreneurship is over. During that era the electronic computer produced a generation of entrepreneurs who eliminated waste and inefficiency in the utilization of time, labor, capital, and resources in all economic enterprises; helped launch new business ventures; changed internal patterns of organizations; helped introduce new products; initiated new technologies of production, distribution and merchandising; and helped create and identify new sources of capital. But the risks of entrepreneurship generated fear and aversion in many people: Workers feared job dislocation, traditional financial institutions feared competition, manufactures feared takeovers, investors feared loss of their capital. Those who subscribed to the egalitarian ideology had a ready explanation for what went wrong: In pursuit of their own selfish interests the new entrepreneurs had put everyone else at risk. As the egalitarians saw it, the fourth age of entrepreneurship was nothing more than a decade of greed, and to fix what had gone wrong there had to be more government regulations and controls that would create a more egalitarian society.

It is possible for the government to create a more egalitarian society through regulations that control enterprise and legislation that redistributes wealth. But this will likely curtail the economic growth of the nation. By 1993 the federal government was spending $11.8 billion on regulation programs. According to the Institute of Policy Innovation, in 1993 the cost of regulation to the economy had risen to $531 billion (Burlington County Times, 1994) Meanwhile, economic recovery, which began in 1991, has been proceeding at half the rate of normal recoveries in terms of productivity, unemployment, and salary increases.

It is significant to note that neither Congress, nor the courts, nor the executive branch stepped in to regulate the stock market after the 1987 crash. Unfettered by government interference the stock market was able to learn from its mistakes and move on to even greater heights in the creation of wealth. From its beginnings, the stock exchange has avoided government regulation. Indeed, the New York Stock Exchange was originally and deliberately created to circumvent government regulation. In 1792, 24 stock brokers gath-

ered under a buttonwood tree on Wall Street to found a private
exchange to elude a New York State prohibition against public stock
auctions. Stock trading remained free from government regulation
until 1934, when Congress, in response to the crash of 1929, created
the Securities and Exchange Commission (SEC).

Although the SEC had broad powers to supervise the securities industry, the Stock Exchange was permitted to police itself. In
1963, the associate director for regulation expressed the SEC's long-
standing position on regulation:

> The only way to regulate an industry as strong and effective and
> with so many bright people as the securities industry was to let
> competition work, as distinguished from regulation. We basically
> were not comfortable with regulation; we didn't trust how it could
> be turned or corrupted. (Blume, Siegel, & Rottenberg, 1993, p. 129)

Ironically, the most significant action ever by the SEC came
in 1978 when it abandoned fixed brokerage commission rates—a
practice that dated back to the 1792 "Buttonwood Agreement." In
abolishing fixed rates the regulator (the SEC) advocated deregulation: Henceforth rates would be set by competition among brokers in
a national market the computer had created.

Unhampered by government regulation, the stock exchange
could modify itself in light of its mistakes, and it could do this faster
and more wisely than any branch of government. Thus, in retrospect,
"the crash was a blessing in disguise," according to William Brodsky,
the president and chief executive of the Chicago Mercantile
Exchange. "The crash created a magnifying glass on how these markets all work and what we needed to do for them to work well together" (*New York Times*, October, 19, 1992). What the magnifying glass
revealed was that the stock exchanges did not have sufficient computer power. This had caused a paralysis of communication, and in
consequence, a breakdown in trading: Without sufficient computer
power brokerage firms became mired in paper orders and telephone
calls; and without sufficient computer power quotes from the
exchanges were tardy, hence meaningless.

Since 1987, the Big Board alone has increased its computer
capacity to comfortably handle 800 million shares a day—up from
about 200 million in 1987. In addition to increased computerization,
the SEC approved the Big Board proposal to use circuit breakers to
restrict computerized program trading. These are imposed whenever
the Dow moves 50 points up or down. Brokerage firms also have
increased their computer power in order to get around trading bottle-
necks. At the time of the crash a customer placing an order would

call a broker, who would fill out a slip of paper and then call a trading desk at the firm with the order. Now, brokers at most brokerage firms can directly place orders using a desktop computer.

WHITHER ENTREPRENEURSHIP?

Although the fourth stage of entrepreneurship appears to have been killed by governmental regulations, in point of fact the entrepreneurship made possible by the electronic computer cannot be stopped by the government. The computer has made capital mobile. Financial assets can be converted into electrical impulses and moved along cables as easily as electricity powers kitchen appliances; additionally those electronic impulses can jump national boundaries by way of satellite transmissions with no more difficulty than do television pictures. Moreover, the free flow of information across national boundaries has made it easier for people to invest over long distances. And once finance capital flows abroad, real capital—plant and equipment, information and brain power—follows. Thus, entrepreneurs can escape any tax increase, any judicial injunction, any agency regulation, the government attempts to impose. The mobility of capital made possible by the electronic computer constrains the power of government to regulate and control it. So, what we have is the emergence of what Richard McKenzie and Dwight Lee called "Quicksilver Capital," and they argue that in this electronic age, whenever a government jurisdiction raises taxes or increases regulations, "capital will depart and the jurisdiction's income will decrease" (1991, p. 101). Of course, national regulators around the world could join forces to create a super-regulatory body. But this is not likely to happen: It would create an incentive for one country to withdraw from such a cartel in hopes of attracting the world's security business.

The upshot of all this is that governments are not only weaker than they once were to control and regulate economic activity, but they are in serious competition with one another to attract capital. Those with the most favorable growth policies will draw capital away from those who remain risk aversive. Very few reporters understand this, and only a few politicians understand it. When Bartlett and Steele asked about an excise tax on securities transactions, Bill Archer, a Republican Congressman from Texas, who serves on the House Ways and Means Committee, replied to the incredulous duo: "I would not support the enactment of such a tax. . . . A transfer tax would cause investors to shift financial transactions to foreign exchanges which do not impose them" (1992, p. 192)

Nevertheless, the entrepreneurial spirit does seem to have diminished—snuffed out by government legislation, regulations, and court cases. Striving for economic growth has been displaced in many quarters by a concern for social justice, for fairness, for equality. Just as aversion to health, safety, and environmental risks brought forth demands for the government to provide equal protection to all, so aversion to economic risk has evoked demands for the government to reduce economic inequalities. Ironically, at the very time more demands are being made on government, we find that politicians are themselves becoming more risk aversive.

PART FOUR

A RISK-AVERSIVE POLITY

11

THE CRISIS OF DEMOCRACY

Many recent analysts of the polity have warned that the faith of the American people in their democratic institutions has declined (see, e.g., Dionne, 1991; Gans, 1991; Grieder, 1991; Morone, 1990). Polls have confirmed such monitions, as has the steady decline in voting in recent national elections. (This was reversed somewhat in the 1992 presidential election.) I suggest that this crisis in democracy has been brought about by the electronic media—television and the computer.

Democracy, in Lincoln's pithy maxim, is government of, by, and for the people. In a representative democracy, officials are elected *by* the people, on behalf *of* the people, *for* the benefit of the people. Voters expect their political officials to serve them, to be responsive to their demands. But prior to the electronic media, American democracy functioned in a sea of ignorance. Except in times of crisis, people did not express or present many demands. This left politicians relatively free to act in ways they thought or believed would best serve their constituents—and win them reelection. The electronic media changed all that.

First, television—by making the public aware of problems and evils heretofore unknown or unacknowledged—raised the number of demands made on the government. Second, the arrival of the computer facilitated and increased the number of surveys and polls of public opinion. At the same time, the computer made possible complex statistical analyses of the data, so that politicians could readily and accurately ascertain the depth, scope, complexity, comprehensiveness, and intensity of public opinion.

The electronic media made it possible for the polity to become more democratic: Now, for the first time, politicians could know what people really wanted, and could, therefore, better satisfy their demands. However, this did not happen. For, once the electronic media had pulled politicians out of the sea of ignorance, they became risk aversive, creating a crisis of democracy.

THE SOCIAL INDICATORS MOVEMENT

Politics today is unthinkable without computers. Yet, computers do not perform the function many had expected them to play in the process of government. Computers, people originally thought, would provide objective, statistical data about society, and thereby facilitate appropriate governmental actions. Where did this idea come from?

In his 1922 book, *Public Opinion*, Walter Lippman wrote:

[T]he printing of comparative statistics of infant mortality is often followed by a reduction in the birth rates of babies. Municipal officials and voters did not have before publication, a place in their picture of the environment for those babies. The statistics made them visible, as visible as if the babies had elected an alderman to air their grievances. (p. 380)

Accurate, objective data about social ills—data on infant mortality, say—enable political leaders to deal effectively with those ills, Lippman argued. Lacking such data, politicians, like all of us, act on stereotypes—on "pictures in our heads we have created or received"—rather than on "direct and certain knowledge." Lippman thought this especially worrisome in a democracy, where governmental decision making is based on public opinion.

He recommended the creation of independent, expert organizations that would make "the unseen facts intelligible to those who have to make the decisions" (p. 31). This would provide a way of overcoming the subjectivism of human organisms stemming from the limitations of individual experience. As long as there was no way of establishing common versions of unseen events—common measures for separate actions—then he warned: "the only image of democracy that would work, even in theory, was one based on an isolated community of people whose political faculties were limited, according to Aristotle's famous maxim, by the range of their vision" (p. 306).

This idea, that a society could produce a quantitative picture of itself, took hold and led in 1929 to the appointment of a Presidential committee that produced a massive report, *Recent Social Trends* (1933). This report prompted President Franklin Roosevelt to establish the National Resources Planning Board and a Central Statistical Board—although nothing much came of either of these organizations.

Of course, every major department of the U.S. Government has long compiled statistics, with the U.S. Census Bureau being the most dominant agency. Ever since 1903, the Bureau of the Census has produced the annual *Statistical Abstract of the United States*. This Annual had actually first appeared in 1879 under the aegis of the Treasury Department. Until 1903, the *Statistical Abstract* was devoted to aspects of foreign trade, shipping, and public finance. When it came under the Bureau of the Census, the *Statistical Abstract* began to include more demographic data: tables on the population by sex, nationality, and race; illiteracy and school attendance; the number of students enrolled in theological, law, and medical schools; and tables showing the number of persons "at least ten years of age, engaged in various "gainful occupations." In time, it added more and more tables on literacy, employment rates, marital conditions, infant mortality, and school enrollments, as well as the population of blind persons, deaf mutes, mental hospital patients, prisoners, and juvenile delinquents.

But the statistics compiled in the yearly statistical abstracts were rarely, if ever, used as the basis for governmental decisions. Part of the reason for this was the absence of any coherent set of social measures that could be used for public analysis. What was needed was some kind of indicators that could allow the society to measure itself and find out in what direction its life was moving.

The introduction of the computer helped to overcome these lacunae in the available statistics. With its ever-expanding storage and processing capacities, the computer could extract from the data what came to be called *social indicators*. In the late 1960s and early 1970s, the U.S. Government and a number of private foundations committed millions of dollars to research on social indicators. Scholars in all areas of social science wrote articles and delivered papers on the topic. The focus, according to R.A. Bauer, one of the promoters of social indicators, was on uncovering "second order consequences: the unforeseen effects on the broad range of social, political, and economic life" (cited in Innes, 1990, p. 94). This required a broad set of measures, not ones designed simply for particular public areas.

In 1966, President Lyndon Johnson set up a group in the Department of Health, Education and Welfare to "develop the necessary social statistical indicators." "With these yardsticks," he said, "we can better measure the distance we have come and plan for the new way ahead" (cited in Innes, p. 95).

The supporters of Johnson's "Great Society" hoped that quantified indicators would provide answers and definitive data for decision making. But when the HEW report, *Toward a Social Report*, appeared in 1969, it took no definitive stands on any issue and made no recommendations.

Although a journal—the *Social Indicators Research Journal: An International and Interdisciplinary Journal for Quality of Life Measurement*"—was launched in 1974, and still continues publication, the social indicators movement never attained the place in government decision making that its advocates had predicted. Several times Senator Walter Mondale proposed legislation to set up a Council of Social Advisors, parallel to the Council of Economic Advisors, who would prepare an annual social report. But such legislation never had support from either a Democratic or Republican administration, nor did it ever get a hearing in the House.

The social indicators movement overlooked the fact that politicians' continual concern with reelection makes them less concerned with objective facts about social conditions and more concerned with their constituents' *opinions* about social conditions.

Here, then, was a true political use for the electronic computer: opinion polls.

OPINION POLLS

Opinion polls had existed in the 19th century, but the first national poll did not take place until 1916, when *The Literary Digest* asked its readers to send in information on public support in their communities for Woodrow Wilson and Charles Evans Hughes. The magazine continued polling until it was humiliated by its 1936 poll which predicted the defeat of Franklin Roosevelt by Alf Landon.

In the mid 1930s, more systematic and scientific polls appeared under the direction of Elmo Roper and George Gallup. Gallup's reports and, later, those of Louis Harris, appeared as syndicated columns and news stories. In the 1960s, with the arrival of the computer, CBS, NBC, and ABC all created in-house polling operations. With the help of computers, news organizations have been able to conduct instant polls to gauge public reaction to events, tracking polls to measure fluctuations in opinions, and panel surveys to study opinion changes. The emergence of computer assisted telephone interviewing (CATI) reduced the time between interview and analysis. As a result, costs were lowered and the number of polls increased. Now, the morning papers can report not only the content of a debate, but also the first public reaction to it.

During the 1992 presidential campaign, George Bush's poll taker conducted 11 national polls, 56 state polls, and 54 focus groups, along with 7,000 continuous polling interviews in October alone. Bill Clinton's pollster did one national poll a week from June to Labor Day, increasing it to three times a week by October. Focus groups were done twice a week until Labor Day and twice a night thereafter (*New York Times*, May 23, 1993). Moreover, polls dominated media coverage of the election campaign. Between July 1 and election day, November 3, 1992, the front page of *USA Today* carried 15 poll-driven stories about the political campaign; The *New York Times* mentioned polls on its front page 53 times during the same period. Twenty different national polls were conducted in the eight days before the election (Crossen, 1994).

Most academic analysts view polls as playing a major role in the conduct of election campaigns, but not in policymaking. Irving Crespi, Director of Media and Public Affairs Research for Total Research Corporation in Princeton, has recently written that, "there is no evidence that public opinion polls have been a decisive factor in the formulation of public policy" (1988, p. 104; see also Erikson, Luttberg, & Tedin, 1980). One frequently referred to study used to support this claim showed that 61% of United States Congressmen never relied on opinion polls (Erikson et al., 1980). But this study was based on data compiled in 1958—before the coming of the computer.

In contrast to the claims of academicians, Richard S. Beal, who served as Director of the Office of Planning and Evaluation in the White House from 1981 to 1983, has written that opinion polls are at the core of presidential decision making. "It may be possible to overstate the role and value of opinion polls in presidential decision making. However, for the modern presidency, the more likely error is to underestimate the availability, influence, and salience of opinion polls on the president and his key advisors" (Beal & Hinckley, 1984, p. 74).

During the first 29 months of the Reagan administration, Beal reveals, the president's long-time pollster, Richard Wirthlin, met with Ronald Reagan more than 25 times to discuss politics and polls, and he delivered memoranda on the results of over 40 public opinion studies to the president's top aides (Beal & Hinckley, 1984, p. 72). In addition, Beal points out, the executive uses polls from the news media and from its own departments, bureaus, and agencies—for example, the Bureau of the Census, the Bureau of Labor Statistics, the Department of Education, and the U.S. Information Agency.

Congress also uses public opinion polls. These are polls conducted by the parties, as well as polls conducted by the Congressmen
themselves. And, of course, they consult polls conducted by the media
and by the various research agencies that serve Congress. They consult public opinion polls in order to ascertain what the public wants
and what it does not want from government.

PUBLIC OPINION POLLS IN THE 1960S AND 1970S

Using computers to find out what voters want made it possible for
government to become more democratic. But, at the very moment
this became possible, the computer-generated public opinion polls
also created the current crisis in democracy. To understand how this
came about, we have to look briefly at how American culture was
affected by that other electronic medium: television.

The arrival of television in the homes of most Americans in
the 1960s heightened the moral sensitivities of the populace to the
unjust and unfair relations that existed in the society—the unfair
relations whites and blacks, and men and women, between old and
young, between rich and poor (Perkinson, 1991). The critical reaction
of the public to what they saw led to widespread demands for the
government to protect these victimized groups. Indeed, television
helped to convert these problems into moral problems and channeled
the clamor to solve them into a moral crusade. In response, legislators passed laws, executives issued decrees, and their appointees created policies, while the courts pronounced decisions—all of which
reduced the victimization of blacks, women, ethnic groups, the young,
and the poor.

During the 1960s and early 1970s, Congress passed the Civil
Rights Act (1965), the Equal Employment Opportunity Act (1972),
and the Immigration and Nationality Act (1965), The Executive
Branch enforced this legislation and strengthened it by executive
orders, such as the Affirmative Action order of 1968. To help the
poor, President Lyndon Johnson launched a war on poverty with a
flurry of legislation, most important of which was the Economic
Opportunity Act of 1964.

By the late 1960s, however, television put on the brakes.
What people now saw on their television screens led many to conclude
that the efforts to redress injustice had gone too far. The "victims"
were demanding too much and resorting to violent means to get it.

Many tried to explain what had happened by reference to the
"Tocqueville Effect." According to this explanation, the diminution of

social injustice in the 1960s and 1970s created a growing rage against the injustices that still remained. Believing that their cause was just and the evils they wanted removed obvious, the protesters could neither understand nor abide public resistance to further social reform. They concluded that this resistance sprang from problems deep in American society itself. It was not simply a matter of unfair laws and policies; it was a matter of the racism, the sexism, and other prejudices deeply seated in the American people. These had to be combated and rooted out. Asking the oppressors to change the laws and the social arrangements was not enough; the oppressors had to be confronted, their prejudices uncovered and overcome. Protest now became a struggle for power, a struggle that took place in public places—where television cameras could film it and show it on the evening news.

The rebellion of youth in the streets of Chicago during the 1968 Democratic Convention; the racial riots for three summers running that took place in almost every major city of the nation; the massive protests against the Vietnam War; and the almost daily confrontations, marches, sit-ins, and acts of civil disobedience on behalf of one or another victimized group—all appeared on people's television screens nightly. This evoked a backlash against protest and protesters and shifted many people from the liberal to the conservative camp. The Gallup Poll on ideological identification ("Are you a liberal or a conservative?") taken yearly since 1938 revealed a sharp change in 1965. Prior to that year, the number of self-identified liberals was always slightly larger than the number of conservatives. In 1965, there was a crossover from liberalism to conservatism, and by 1970, self-identified conservatives outnumbered liberals by 64% (Robinson & Heishman, 1984) In another poll taken in 1964, about 40% of the moderates and conservatives identified themselves as one-time liberals, and most pinpointed their change as coming after 1963 (Phillips, 1993).

One of the results of this shift toward conservatism was the election of Richard Nixon in 1968. As Commander-in-Chief, Nixon escalated the war in Vietnam and de-escalated the war on poverty. Nixon also opposed government action to enforce racial integration, such as federally mandated busing, affirmative action (he called it quotas), and federally established timetables for school integration. Other signs of political reaction were the defeat of the Equal Rights Amendment and the diminution of both federal and state legislation to combat social injustice.

The most dramatic sign of the change in public opinion was the devastating defeat of the Democratic candidate in the 1972 presidential election. This debacle can be traced back to the Democratic Convention in Chicago four years earlier. At that 1968 Democratic

Convention, Hubert Humphrey won the nomination in spite of his not having won a single primary victory. This infuriated the reformers and prompted them to take control of the party's rule-making process through a commission headed by Senator George McGovern.

Insisting on participatory democracy, the commission introduced affirmative action in the selection of convention delegates, thereby increasing the number of black, Latino, Asian, female, and youth representatives. It further insisted that primaries and open caucuses, not party bosses, should dominate the nominating process.

Because he understood these new rules best, George McGovern threw his hat into the ring early and won enough delegates prior to the 1972 convention to secure the nomination. The reformers also succeeded in constructing a Democratic party platform committed to continuing social reform, which came to be called the "rights revolution." The 1972 platform contained separate planks on the rights of the poor, American Indians, the physically disabled, the mentally retarded, the elderly, veterans, women, and children It also included "the right to be different, to maintain a cultural or ethnic heritage or lifestyle, without being forced into a compelled homogeneity" (Edsall & Edsall, 1991, p. 95).

The Democratic campaign for a substantial redistribution of power, privilege, wealth, status, cultural authority, government resources, and legal protection was overwhelmingly rejected by voters in the 1972 election. George McGovern lost every state in the union, except Massachusetts.

Shortly after the Republican landslide victory, the Watergate break-in scandal forced Richard Nixon to resign from the presidency. This discredited the conservative movement and opened the way for the moral presidency of Jimmy Carter, who promised: "I'll never lie to you."

But Carter was no liberal. He excoriated the welfare system for damaging work and family values, and he opposed the federal bureaucracy. Except for the areas of occupational health and safety, the environment, and consumer protection, very little social legislation came out of the Carter administration. Jimmy Carter spent most of his time as President coping with the faltering economy—rising interest rates, soaring inflation, more and more unemployment; and with deteriorating foreign affairs—the oil embargo, the Soviet Union's invasion of Afghanistan, and the Iran hostage crisis.

The absence of responsive administrations in the White House after 1968 prompted a shift in the liberal, or egalitarian, quest for social justice. Performers now appealed to the federal courts, most of which were now staffed by judges appointed in the more egalitarian '60s. And because they are appointed, not elected, federal judges did not have to worry about public opinion. During both the Nixon and Carter administrations, the Supreme Court issued a number of decisions that advanced the egalitarian agenda. For example, the Court sanctioned busing (*Swann v. Charlotte-Mecklenberg* [1971], and *Keyes v. School District No. 1*, Denver, Colorado [1973]); supported abortion (*Roe v. Wade* [1973]); promoted student rights (*Tinker v. Des Moines Independent Community School District* [1969], *Goss v. Lopez* [1975]); approved the deinstitutionalization of the mentally ill (*O'Connor v. Donaldson* [1975]); and overturned vagrancy laws (*Papachristou v. City of Jacksonville* [1972]).

Not only the Supreme Court, but the lower federal courts also furthered the agenda of the egalitarian reformers. The number of civil cases filed in U.S. District Courts rose from under 50 thousand in 1960 to almost 300,000 by the end of the 1980s (Ginsberg & Shefter, 1990). Throughout the nation, women's groups, gay groups, and groups who served as advocates for the mentally impaired, for prisoners, for immigrants, and for accused criminals, all used the federal courts to assault existing laws, policies, practices, procedures, and arrangements that denied them social justice. The statistics reveal how successful they were.

First, the women's rights movement made women more autonomous and less dependent on man: They entered the work force in greater numbers, more readily divorced their spouses, had more abortions, and had more children out of wedlock.

- Labor force participation among married women grew from 35.7% in 1965 to 50.7% in 1980.
- Reported abortions rose from 586,800 in 1972 to 1.2 million in 1976.
- For whites, the illegitimacy rate rose from 5.7% of all live births in 1970 to 11% in 1980; for blacks, the rate went from 37.6% to 55.2%.

Second, the movement to secure rights for accused criminals made their prosecution and incarceration more difficult. The diminution in the likelihood of punishment and the failure to incapacitate criminals led to an increase in criminal activity.

- Reported crimes rose from 3.38 million in 1960 to 13.4 million in 1980—a 296% increase.
- Reported violent crimes (murder, robbery, assault, and rape) increased from 288,000 in 1960 to 1.3 million in 1990—a 367% increase.

- After holding steady at approximately 200,000 for 15 years, the number of people in prisons increased to 400,000 by 1982.

Third, the movement to guarantee immigration rights made it more difficult to restrict immigrants from entering the United States, more difficult to exclude them from social and welfare services, and more difficult to expatriate them for any reason. This reduction o9f such interdictions resulted in an increase in immigration.

- The total number of legal immigrants and refugees from Central and South America rose from 183,717 in the 1950s to 751,060 in the 1960s, and to 1,555,697 in the 1970s.
- The total number of Asian immigrants increased from 186,671 in the 1950s to 751,060 in the 1960s, and to 1,555,697 in the 1970s. The total Asian population grew from 1.34 million in 1970 to 7.3 million in 1990.

The statistics compiled and dutifully reported in the press and on radio and television confirmed the feelings of most Americans that the society was rapidly changing. Whether the change was good or bad depended on one's ideology: Egalitarians regarded the changes as good, as social progress; individualists saw them as bad, as social decay.

THE COMPUTER AND IDEOLOGICAL POLARIZATION

So long as citizens had remained ignorant of much that was going on in the society, and so long as politicians had remained ignorant of what people wanted from government, most everyone had continued to assume that most or all Americans pretty much subscribed to the same set of liberal ideals, values, and attitudes (Hartz, 1955). The electronic media undermined such assumptions about public opinion.

As a result of watching television—which visually presents what is going on in the society—public opinion in America became markedly polarized. Those with an egalitarian outlook increasingly demanded that the government help the victims depicted nightly on television screens—the victims of racism, sexism, and ethnic discrimination. Those with an individualist outlook blamed the victims and demanded that the government not encourage the deviant behavior viewed nightly on television screens—deviant behavior promoted by black militants, feminists, homosexuals, and criminals. Those Americans whose opinions had heretofore placed them in the center now began to tilt one way or the other, becoming more ideologically egalitarian, or more ideologically individualist. In their exhaustive study of the American voter, Norman Nie, Sidney Verba, and John Petrocik found far fewer people in the centrist category in 1973 than in 1956, and they found a large growth in leftist and rightist beliefs during the same time period (Nie, Verba, & Petrocik, 1979).

Since the 1960s, computer-conducted polls have intensified polarization by asking people to evaluate public policies in terms of their ideologies. Then, by encoding them in percentages, in graphs, and in charts, the computer hardened and calcified that polarization of society into egalitarian and individualist camps. Armed with these statistics, which purported to describe the social reality ("Numbers don't lie, do they?"), proponents of both sides could "see through" the arguments of the other side. Thus, individualists "saw through" the pleas made by egalitarians for equality, fairness, and progress. Such pleas, the individualists explained, were no more than masked attacks on religion, morality, and family values. The egalitarians, in turn, "saw through" the pleas made by individualists for maintaining traditional values, free enterprise, and self-reliance. Such pleas, the egalitarians explained, were no more than attacks on equality, fairness, and progress.

In the late 1970s, the cultural war between individualists and egalitarians moved into the economic sphere when individualists began to attack the egalitarian spending policies that had first appeared in the 1960s.

Although the ideological individualists had succeeded in capturing the White House in 1968 and had all but eliminated new egalitarian legislation throughout the 1970s—even during the Democratic Carter years—the laws passed earlier in the 1960s continued in force, becoming more and more costly to maintain, especially the welfare benefits for the poor.

- From 1965 to 1970, the number of households on welfare more than doubled, reaching 2,208,000, and then grew another million by 1975, reaching 3,498,000.
- From 1965 to 1975, the number of families receiving benefits under Aid to Families with Dependent Children (AFDC) grew by 237%.
- The food stamp program, which provided benefits to 400,000 in 1965, increased to 17.1 million recipients in 1975.

The increase in welfare payments of all kinds was the direct result of the decline in economic growth since the 1960s. When the economy stopped growing unemployment rose and welfare payments increased. Moreover, economic stagnation was now partnered with rising inflation—a condition diagnosed as "stagflation." Inflation, in turn, caused "bracket creep" among the employed, especially the lower and middle classes, who found that their increased wages ratcheted them into higher marginal tax rates. To add to these tax woes, Congress approved higher social security taxes, raising the maximum annual security tax by 473%.

Faced with rising taxes and rising government spending on welfare, some 82% of Americans polled in 1978 thought that the government was "spending too much." This poll came on the heels of another conducted the previous year in which 60% said that the federal income tax was unfair (Sussman, 1988).

It was not surprising, then, that the late 1970s saw the beginning of a tax revolt. It began in California in 1978 when voters, by a margin of 2 to 1, ratified Proposition 13, which cut property taxes by more than $6 billion. This was followed by a wave of tax cutting and tax referenda in some 18 other states in the next four years. In 1980 Ronald Reagan swept into the White House vowing to get the government off the people's backs by promising to reduce taxes, expenditures, and federal regulation of business and industry.

The Reagan victory in 1980 reflected not only an increased dissatisfaction with Federal economic policies, but also an increased dissatisfaction with what ideological individualists called *social deviance*, which they claimed the government had helped to create. This second wave of conservative protest against the increased power of the federal government was spearheaded by what came to be called the *religious right*, a group best described as ideological hierarchs.

The involvement of Christian fundamentalists in politics came about directly as a reaction to a decision made in 1978 by the IRS Commissioner during the Carter administration that denied tax exempt status to segregated Christian private schools in the south. The "Moral Majority," created in 1979, drew its staff and legal resources from the people who ran those Christian schools. At least 25 of the first 50 state chairmen of the Moral Majority were affiliated with fundamentalist churches that sponsored Christian academies (Edsall & Edsall, 1991).

What enabled the Moral Majority to emerge so rapidly as a player in national politics was its utilization of the electronic computer. According to fund-raiser Richard Viguerie, "Direct mail is the life blood of the right." Using the mailing lists of 250,000 donors to Jerry Falwell's "Old Time Gospel Hour," the Moral Majority raised $1 million in one month. By the middle of 1980, the organization claimed a membership of 300,000. The computer facilitated the raising of money and the propagation of ideas, as well as the recruiting of activists and the mobilizing of supporters.

The Moral Majority became the cornerstone of what came to be called the *new right*, giving added political focus to the cultural concern of conservatives. Whereas individualist conservatives in the past had typically stressed economic and foreign policy issues, the ideological hierarchs who made up the new right broadened conservative concerns to social issues—busing, abortion, pornography, education, quotas, and traditional values.

When he ran successfully for President in 1980, Ronald Reagan not only vowed to reduce governmental interference in the economy but also gave his support to the agenda of the new right: anti-abortion, pro-prayer in school, anti-pornography, anti-busing, and pro-family values.

In the first half of his first term, Reagan set out to cut taxes, reduce inflation, slash social programs, increase defense outlays, reduce federal regulatory controls over business, and diminish federal efforts on behalf of blacks and other minorities. He did obtain a tax cut and significantly increased defense outlays, but the rest of his legislative program was opposed by groups who successfully lobbied Congress to defend social entitlement programs and to retain environmental regulation on business. At the same time, the Federal Reserve Board raised interest rates so high that the economy went into a recession. The upshot was an enormous increase in the federal deficit.

Although Reagan won reelection in 1984 by 59% of the popular vote, while carrying 49 states, it was obvious that the nation remained polarized on social and economic issues and therefore at odds on the matter of more government versus less government. This increased ideological polarization of the electorate is at the root of the crisis of American democracy

Our society remains deeply divided over what to do about many problems: race and gender, poverty and crime, abortion and illegitimacy, education and the schools, welfare and national defense, environmentalism and economic growth, and violence and social justice—to mention but a few. On all these issues each side blames the policies of the other side for putting democracy at risk. It is this aversion to risk that has exacerbated the intensity of the opposition between conservatives (a group that includes both ideological individualists and ideological hierarchists) and liberals (ideological egalitarians).

Yet, ideological polarization has, to some extent, always been with us; in itself it does not constitute a crisis of democracy. It is the computer that has brought this polarization to center stage and, thus, the crisis of American democracy. The computer generates polls and surveys of public opinion duly encoded in charts, tables, and graphs—all of which heighten politicians' awareness of the polarized opinions Americans hold on the ideological issues confronting the society.

Politicians will not, cannot, act in ways that risk their own reelection. So, when confronted with conflicting demands from voters—backed by computer-generated numbers—many politicians become cautious. Instead of dealing with the issues that divide the society, they instead try to accurately ascertain and reflect the opinions of their own constituents in order to win reelection. Instead of governing, they become permanent candidates.

12

THE RISE OF THE PERMANENT CANDIDATE

The rise of the permanent candidate in American politics has to be viewed in the context of Watergate. In 1974, the year Richard Nixon was driven from the White House by the Watergate scandal, Congress challenged the Presidency as an institution by seizing powers it had never before possessed. In reaction to its own budget conflict with President Nixon, Congress passed the Budget and Improvement Control Act of 1974, to bar future presidents from refusing to spend what Congress had voted, thereby giving legislators much more control over federal spending. That law also set up the Congressional Budget Office (CBO) to produce independent analyses of the economy and the budget. This move by Congress to emulate the Office of Management and Budget (OMB) and the Council of Economic Advisors (both of which served the president), greatly enhanced the power of the legislative branch by providing it with more computerized data and computer-generated information about the economy and the society than it had access to heretofore. To further weaken the monopoly the executive branch had on information, Congress also expanded other existing support agencies during those post-Watergate years: the Congressional Research Service, the Office of Technology and Assessment, and the General Accounting Office.

In retrospect, this increase in the amount of computer generated information made available to congressmen helped to undermine the legislative branch of government.

THE DECLINE OF THE LEGISLATOR

One immediate consequence of the increased amount of information and data now available to Congress was to make the old standing committee system unworkable. To effectively handle all the available information, Congress had to increase the number of its committees. The move to expand the number of committees was sparked by the 75 Democratic "Watergate Babies" elected to the House in 1974. These newcomers assaulted the traditional seniority system, deposing the chairmen of the powerful standing committees and creating numerous subcommittees, each of which took charge of a slice of federal policy. The 22 standing committees were split into 172 subcommittees, the chairmen of each of which could bargain with high officials, push their pet ideas, and grab publicity. This dispersal of power was facilitated by the adoption of a "subcommittee bill of rights."

Such reforms balkanized Congressional power and made the passage of legislation a veritable steeplechase. For, after increasing the number of its committees, the House adopted the policy of multiple referral. Prior to 1974, the Speaker had been required to assign legislation to the single committee that had predominate jurisdiction for the content of a bill. Now the Speaker could send legislation to committees jointly or sequentially, or by splitting it into parts. Such a policy not only undermined the autonomy of a committee, it increased the potential for conflict. Moreover, it made passage of any complex legislation difficult and time-consuming. When President Carter submitted his energy bill to Congress in 1978, it had to pass through 22 different Congressional committees.

A second immediate consequence of the increase in computer-generated information available to Congress was the dramatic increase in Congressional staff. In the wake of the increased information that computers now made available, members of Congress soon realized they needed help. Increasingly, they had to rely on their staff to analyze proposed legislation. In 1975 Congressman Wayne Hayes—who was both Chairman of the Democratic National Committee and Chairman of the House Administration Committee— granted all House members larger allowances. This enabled them to travel home more frequently, send more mail to their constituents, and enlarge their staffs.

During the 1970s, House staffs nearly tripled in size, while Senate staffs doubled. By 1989, the average representative had a staff budget of about $400,000, which paid for an average of 17 staffers. Many of the staff workers conducted investigations, and reviewed, analyzed, and wrote legislation. Others handled inquiries, complaints, and problems of constituents. These case workers checked on social security payments, inquired about relatives in the armed services, helped veterans get medical care, facilitated the awarding of grants, contracts and loans to their constituents, and, in general, converted Congressmen from legislators into ombudsmen. The computerized Member Information Network helped by providing Congressmen and their staffs with census information, lists of grants, contracts, loans, and direct payments already given out, and information about eligibility, restrictions, and the application process.

At the same time that stafflation diverted congressmen's attention from legislating, it actually contributed to the increase in the amount of legislation they had to deal with. Because staffers are bright, young, aggressive, ambitious, full of ideas, and astute enough to know that their careers depend on expanding the turf and power of their bosses, they inevitably become entrepreneurial. They seek out new policy initiatives for which their bosses can gain credit and win reelection. This increases the workload of the members of Congress: more committee and subcommittee meetings, more hearings, and more amendments to consider. Yet this increase in workload did not increase the work *product* of Congress. According to Michael Malbin, Congress over the past decades has passed fewer public bills of greater than average length. (The 1970 Clean Air Act occupied a mere 47 pages in the United States Code; its renewal in 1990 consumed more than 200 fine-print pages in the *Congressional Record*, *(New York Times*, October 16, 1994, p. E6). Moreover, a Congressional Commission on Administrative Review found a decline in the time members of Congress spend on "legislation, research, and reading: down from one day a week in 1965 to an average of eleven minutes per day in 1977" (Malbin, 1980, p. 243).

The overburdened member of Congress often, literally, does not know what he or she is doing. On an average day each has two, sometimes three, simultaneous committee hearings, as well as floor votes and issues caucuses. As Hedrick Smith (1988) describes it: "He will dart into one hearing, get a quick fill-in from his staffer, inject his ten minutes worth, and rush on to the next event, often told by an aide how to vote as he rushes to the floor" (p. 382). It is the staff specialist, not the Congressman, who understands the substance of the policy issues. "You skate along the surface of things," Senator William Cohen conceded. "More and more you are dependent on your staff" (cited in Smith, 1988, p. 284). The knowledgeability and centrality of the nonelected Congressional staff are corroborated by the fact that both lobbyists and reporters seek them out to obtain accurate insight and information about legislation (Malbin, 1980).

Over and beyond the role the Congressional staff plays in the formation of policy is the substantive impact it has through its role in negotiations. Staff-to-staff negotiations short circuit deliberations and direct conversation among Congressmen. In an op-ed piece published in the *New York Times*, entitled: "Why I am leaving the Senate," David Boren wrote: "There was no time for reflection, no time to exchange ideas with fellow senators. Too often attempts to talk with another senator about teaming up on a bill or amendment were met with "I can't talk now, but have your staff person call my staff to talk about it" (May 13, 1994).

By leaving negotiations to staff technicians, members of Congress not only lose touch with the details of policy formation, they fail to represent their constituents. They become spokespersons for general positions rather than hands-on experts. And the legislation that results from staff negotiations is always a compromise among competing self-interested parties, which means that the final product is inevitably so complex that it can only be understood by an expert. Power has shifted to staffers, away from the elected representatives of the people.

Take Section 89 of the 1986 tax bill. This was supposed to weed out discrimination in employment-benefit plans—plans where an employer offered a more generous package to some than to others. Under the provision that became law, companies could still offer sweeter benefits to some of their paid employees, but those employees had to pay income tax on the extra perks. Section 89 set up a maze of complicated tests a company had to pass to prove it was not providing discriminatory benefits. Tax attorneys, accountants, and small businessmen complained furiously about the complexity and burden of the provision. It had been designed by staffers of the House Ways and Means Committee. "The organized rules were wildly too complex," one staff person admitted. "We didn't pick up on it." Later, the House voted to repeal Section 89 (Wolpe, 1990, p. 96).

The surfeit of information the computer supplied to congressmen forced them to increase the number of committees in the House and the number of staff. Both these moves made it more difficult for them to function as legislators. Perhaps an even more important and related consequence of the information explosion was to loosen the discipline of members of Congress.

THE EMERGENCE OF THE PERMANENT CANDIDATE

Members of Congress can no longer be disciplined by the President, by the party, by Committee Chairs, nor by Congressional leaders.

Each member of Congress is on his or her own, free to act in ways designed to secure reelection. There is not only less party loyalty, less subservience to committee chairs and party leaders, there is also less concern with the national interest. In pursuit of their own agendas, independent members of Congress have launched more filibusters than ever before in the history of Congress and have increasingly blocked votes on legislation with endless amendments from the floor.

Now committee chairs have to win over each member individually. And to secure each member's support, the proposed legislation has to be modified to provide benefits for the interests or constituencies each member represents. This raises the costs of government programs and diffuses their impact. Thus, to secure passage of the 1981 tax cut, the Reagan administration had to go support shopping—by offering major exemptions and deductions to a host of special interests, including manufacturers, small businesses, and the oil industry. According to David Stockman, this almost doubled the cost to the treasury of the tax cut proposal and contributed heavily to subsequent budget deficits (Stockman, 1986).

In addition to support shopping, those seeking to pass legislation must accept the burden shifting many members of Congress insist on. This happens when members demand that, in exchange for their support, the interests for whom they speak be relieved of the costs and burdens associated with the new programs. Benjamin Ginsberg and Martin Shefter point out that this is what happened to the Bush administration's initial plan for resolving the crisis in the Savings and Loan (S&L) industry. That plan called for imposing a fee on S&L deposits. But the industry and the Congressional spokespeople for the industry objected and insisted that general tax revenues finance the cost of the (then-estimated) $150 billion bailout—thus shifting the burden to the general public (Ginsberg & Shefter, 1990).

Another way unfettered members of Congress obstruct the formulation of public policy is by using legislative proposals as weapons of political combat to attack or undermine their enemies, whether personal, party, or institutional. Thus, Republicans have accepted the economic risk of unprecedented deficits because of the constraints these deficits impose on the Democrats. Likewise, Congressional Democrats oppose military spending because the defense establishment is a bastion of the Republicans.

As result of the practices of the last 20 years—support shopping, burden shifting, and weapon sharpening—the legislative process has been seriously deadlocked by politicians solely concerned with their own reelection, even at the cost of political paralysis. As Congressman Charles Schumer put it: "Congress has become atomistic. In the House, we are 435 little atoms bouncing off each other, colliding and influencing each other but not in a very coherent way. There used to be much more structure. But now there is no bonding that holds the atoms together" (cited in Smith, 1988, p. 39).

Once unfettered, members of Congress found themselves largely responsible for their own reelection. In this constant campaign they turned to computer technology.

Legislators enjoy free mailings, and that old-fashioned Congressional privilege has been adopted to modern computer technology. Today, Senators and House members use high-speed laser printers, automated letter folders, and computerized mass mailing systems. They use computers to locate friendly or swing voters for carefully targeted messages. By using computers to segment the market, politicians can now go after people who have single-issue goals and motivations. By using computer lists of licensed drivers, membership lists of organizations, and mail-in questionnaires, Congressmen can identify and segment voters into age groups, ethnic groups, religious groups, as well as interest and issue groups. They can narrow-cast targeted mail to tell people what they want to hear: "Knowing your interest in a balanced budget, I want you to know about this . . ." or, "As a retired person, I thought you would be concerned about . . ."

To accomplish these mail-marketing techniques, Senators can use the Senate Computer Center with its staff of 180, which is financed by approximately $32 million of taxpayers' money. The computers in the Center store the names, addresses, and interests of millions of voters, broken down into more than 3,300 categories. And its laser printers can roll out 50,000 letters daily—predesigned paragraph by paragraph to personalize them for targeted audiences. Many contain personalized references that repeat the person's name, hometown, interests, or group. All use an ink that disguises that the signature was done by a machine (Smith, 1988). (Some use a special ink that will smudge as if someone did, in fact, sign it.)

The efforts of members of Congress to keep in touch with and to show their constituents that they care generate a staggering amount of mail—920 million pieces in 1984 alone, which was more than double the volume four years earlier. And the amount of mail Congress sends out rises sharply in election years: According to *Roll Call*, House members spent $5.9 million on franked mail in the first quarter of 1991; but in the first quarter of 1992—an election year— they spent $10.7 million, an increase of 82%. In one two-day period in the Spring of 1992, members of the House churned out 58 million pieces of franked mail (cited in Will, 1992).

Perhaps even more important to incumbents today are prepackaged electronic press releases: videotapes for television outlets and audiotapes for radio stations. These often go on the air as straight news reports without any indication that Congressional politicians originated them or that taxpayer dollars usually paid for them. Both parties have multimillion dollar media complexes and studios in Capitol Hill, equipped with state of the art videotape recorders, mixers, modulators, and electronic switching and blending machines to mix sight and sound, live interviews, and fancy graphics.

The Senate Republican Conference has studios, film editing rooms, and disks on the roof to provide satellite feeds for Senators. This means that Senators can do live two-way press conferences, town meetings, and call-in shows. The Conference gets a taxpayer subsidy of over half a million dollars annually.

To wage their constant campaign for reelection, Congressmen need money, lots of money. Most of it they obtain from lobbyists. In 1974, in reaction to the taint of Nixon's campaign slush funds, Congress voted for strict public financing of presidential elections, coupled with strict limitations on individual contributions to campaigns. But it refused to allow public subsidies for congressional races, thereby strengthening the role of Political Action Committees (PACs). Most of the money from lobbyists is given through PACs, and it is substantial. Contributions from PACs to all candidates for the House and Senate rose from $12.5 million in 1974 to $139.4 million in 1986 (Sorauf, 1988). Corporate PACs who raise money and make contributions to the election campaigns of candidates friendly to corporate interests rose from 89 in 1974 to 1,779 in 1987.

By 1987, there were 23,001 registered lobbyists in Washington—a ratio of 43 to 1 for each member of the House and Senate. Not all lobbyists are registered, so another indication of how their numbers have increased is the number of corporations with offices in Washington: up from 100 in 1968 to 1,300 by 1986.

There are, of course, lobbyists from fields other than business and industry. There are public interest lobby groups and environmental lobby groups. Labor unions lobby, as do physicians and teachers. Foreign governments have their lobbyists, as do blacks and all ethnic groups. Senior citizens have lobbyists, as do sportsmen. Organized anti-vivisectionists, anti-abortionists, and anti-pornography groups lobby, as do their organized opponents. There are also lobbying firms who can be hired by individuals or groups to do their work for them. A current directory of Washington lobbyists estimates that 1,500 individual corporations have their own lobbyists, and 2,200 associations and unions also have permanent offices in the area.

The coming of the computer lowered the costs of organizing and maintaining a lobby group. Computerized membership lists, computerized mailing, and computer networking all significantly reduced the amount of time, energy, and money needed to gather people into an association that could have considerable clout. Moreover, the computer has reduced reaction time. First, with the help of computer network services like "Legi-Slate" and "Washington Alert Service," lobby groups can immediately access and search the text of bills before Congress, the committee calendars, the voting records of individual congressmen, and databases containing political contributions. Second, armed with information about what is going on, lobbyists can use the computer to marshal an immediate response from their members. In March 1985, for example, an amendment was attached to an antitrust bill that the National League of Cities (NLC) opposed because they considered it harmful to urban concerns. The NLC posted an immediate electronic bulletin on their computer network asking local municipal officials to call their congressmen to voice their opposition. The amendment was defeated (Abrahamson, Arterton, & Orren, 1988).

In the electronic age the costs of belonging to an interest or lobbying group have diminished. That is, one does not have to spend evenings stuffing envelopes, telephoning supporters, or housecalling. The member merely sends in his or her name and some money—the computer handles everything else. So, understandably, more people belong to interest groups. According to a 1990 survey conducted by the American Society of Association Executives, 7 out of 10 Americans belong to at least one association that lobbies in Washington. The variety and scope of these associations are staggering—so broad and deep that Senator Richard Lugar of Indiana declared "there is very little space left."

In a speech delivered in 1992, Senator Lugar admitted

> I have regularly on Tuesday as many as fifteen constituent groups from Indiana, all of whom have been revved up by some skillful person, employed for that purpose in Washington, to cite bills that they don't understand, have never heard of prior to that time, but with a scoresheet to report back to headquarters, whether I am for or against. It is so routine, it is so fierce, it goes on every week every year, that, you know, at some point you [can't be] immune to it. You try to be responsive. (cited in Abrahamson et al., 1988, p. 49)

The reason why Congressmen cannot be immune to the demands of lobbyists is simply that they need their money for reelection. In the 1985-86 general election, for example, the National Conservative PAC donated $9.3 million; the Realtors PAC, $6 million; the American Medical Association PAC, $5.4 million; and the National Rifle Association Political Victory Fund, $4.7 million.

PACs are limited to contributing $5,000 per candidate per election. But because they travel in herds and operate under the guidance of PAC strategists who advise all corporate, all labor, or all industry-wide individual PACs where to put their money, the total contributions from PACs can be enormous.

Although PAC contributions are restricted by law to "political purposes"—that is, campaign contributions—it is clear to most that they are often used to buy influence and build good will for legislative purposes. This is evident from the fact that some PACs—for example, GE in the 1984 election—give money to incumbents who have no opponents in the election; as well as from the fact that PACs commonly give money to help winning candidates liquidate campaign debts after elections.

Critics accuse lobbyists of destroying the electoral process by buying votes. Lobbyists respond that they are simply buying access—seeking a chance to make their case. Access is important, because a Congressman's time is always limited. Moreover, they point out that lobbyists stay away from those legislators clearly against them and their programs. Attempts at conversion are most likely to boomerang. So, labor PACs support pro-labor Congressmen, corporate PACs, pro-business types, farm PACs give money to their allies; and so on.

What do lobbyists want?

Their fundamental interest is in transferring resources. They lobby to have society divert more resources to some activity that they like and away from some activity they do not like. These transfers take many different forms.

Tax codes are one of the main forms of transfer. Groups lobby for taxes on activities they do not like. The anti-smoking and anti-drinking groups lobby for higher liquor and cigarette taxes. At the same time groups lobby for tax breaks on activities they favor. Realtors and Home Owners associations lobby for tax breaks for property owners. As a result of thousands of groups clamoring for tax breaks, Congress revised the federal tax code eight times between 1981 and 1990. Just in the five years after the 1986 tax reform, Congress made about 5,400 changes to it through 27 different pieces of legislation.

Subsidies are another form of transfer seeking: Associations representing farmers, the elderly, the disabled, or many other groups, all lobby for subsidies for their members. Associations also lobby for policies and laws that protect their members from competition: these take the form of tariffs, or import quotas that protect manufacturers; or they take the form of minimum wage laws and job replacement laws that protect workers; or licensing laws that protect the practitioners of various occupations and professions. Transfers can also be secured through legal mandates, like seat-belt laws sought by seat-belt manufacturers, or mandatory insurance sought by insurance companies.

Almost every lobby group always believes it is doing good: What it seeks is for the common good—whether it is subsidies, higher tariffs, higher taxes, tax breaks, restrictions on polluters, safety rules, or prohibitions on drugs. Fueled by moral outrage and deep convictions, every lobby group insists on the righteousness of its cause—"If our competitors are subsidized (or have tax breaks, or a tariff on foreign competition) then it is only fair to subsidize us." Moreover, as every government program generates an entrenched lobby that will not go away, this means that once a lobby group secures a transfer, it stays on the books—"We need federal money (or federal jobs, or federal contracts) because, having received it for all these years, we can't get along without."

The upshot of the increased transfer seeking of lobby groups has been a phenomenal growth in government programs that cannot be withdrawn and are difficult to cut down. If Congress tries to trim a program, the interest groups complain bitterly and fight hard. The Reagan administration set out to kill domestic programs, but during its eight years in office a grand total of four major programs (government revenue sharing, urban development action grants, the synthetic fuel program, and the Clinch River breeder reactor) actually got killed. In 1989, the Bush administration proposed ending 246 federal programs—none of them very large. Congress eliminated only eight (Rauch, 1994).

This proliferation of government programs that never die nor ever diminish, has deepened the crisis of democracy, creating a condition Jonathan Rauch calls "demosclerosis": the government's progressive loss of the ability to adapt (1994). It is not that Congress does nothing, Rauch points out, but that it continues to authorize new transfers—adding them to what already exists. Because established programs are never eliminated, nor even modified, innovative new programs never appear, and financial resources are increasingly drained.

Lobbyists engaged in transfer seeking have not only expanded government, they are also helping to undermine representative government. PACs do not buy and own members of congress, but they do distort their perspectives by forcing each one to think parochially. Like a laser beam, PAC money helps a particular interest group exercise powerful influence on the side of an issue it cares about. Other interests have less influence, hence other issues are ignored. Moreover, as much of the PAC money comes from state organizations, members of Congress sometimes become more responsive to special interests than to their own constituents. A clear example of this was the 1986 tax bill which contained favorable provisions for the oil and timber industries, the insurance industry, the smokestack industries, and small businesses—all of which contributed millions of dollars to the members of the Senate Finance Committee and the House Ways and Means Committee.

Lobbyists are able to wield so much influence over members of congress because, in addition to providing money to elected officials, lobbyists supply those in congress with information on issues, and questions to ask at hearings, They help write speeches and op-ed articles for members, and often help subcommittee staff write legislation. The lobbyists invariably know more about the subject than either the members or their staffs. As one lobbyist explained: "There are very arcane, very turgid, complications of the tax code, and members of their staffs often are not familiar with how they apply to the industry as we are. So, if you've got entree there and you understand the process and you're present, you can influence the specific drafting of those proposals. Staff and others will come out and seek you out in the halls and say 'we're on the passive-loss provision, and this is the material-participation that the staff is proposing. Does that work? Does that solve your problem? And if not, how can we correct it?" (Smith, 1988, pp. 235-236).

The computer has made possible one other way for lobbyists to influence Congress. They buy or create grassroots movements. They plant, maintain, and orchestrate coalitions of voters to exert pressure on elected officials. By using computers, lobbyists can target demographic groups based on such characteristics as the kinds of home, cars, clothes, magazines, tapes, discs, and gadgets people buy. Each group has political reactions that are fairly predictable, so the right message can be sent to the right people through telephone, mail, or mailgram. To facilitate targeted mailings, commercial firms sell computer tapes matching members of Congress (with their sub-committees and issue specializations) with lists of voters collated by interest and district. Some trade associations collect advance proxies from their members and have their names on computers, ready for generating instant mass mailings. The life insurance lobby has developed kits that include pretyped letters addressed to Congressmen that have varied texts, personalized letterheads, on different colors of stationery—to avoid the appearance of mass production.

Congress is now buried in an avalanche of computer generated mail organized by lobbies. In 1972, the House of Representatives received 14.6 million pieces of mail. By 1985, it had increased to more than 225 million pieces—an average of more than half a million

pieces a year per member. Sometimes lobby groups target a particular day and truck in computerized mail all at once to a key member of
Congress, like the House Speaker. On several occasions, House
Speaker Tip O'Neill received 5 million pieces of mail in a single day
(Smith, 1988). The record was set in Summer 1985 when three trac-
tor-trailer trucks delivered 15 to 18 million pieces. Even though the
pressure from the grassroots looks contrived, elected officials cannot
ignore it. Mass mail reveals organizational force, and that can threat-
en a politician's reelection. And make no mistake about it: Reelection
is the primary concern of incumbent politicians.

Since 1974, the first election after the scandals of Watergate,
the reelection of incumbents has steadily increased. In the 1990 election, over 96% of those in the House seeking reelection were returned
to office, and the rate for the Senate was 96.7%. In the 1992 election,
93% of the House incumbents were reelected.

Incumbents win reelection to Congress because they have
become permanent candidates. Instead of governing, they spend most
of their time and energy chasing publicity, doing favors, and pork-
barrel work—all aimed at getting support and money for their campaigns. Thomas Eagleton, just before he retired from the Senate,
gave this estimate to a journalist: "I would say that an incumbent
Senator in a hotly contested reelection campaign would devote seven-
ty to eighty percent of his personal time, effort, thought, and worry-
ing to fundraising for the last two years of a six year term" (Smith,
1988, p. 158).

Can anything be done to get politicians to govern instead of
becoming permanent candidates?

Changes in campaign financing making politicians less
dependent on interest groups and lobby groups for funds might help.
More deregulation would help, too, by stripping Congress of the possibility of doing favors for special interest groups. More decentraliza-
tion would accomplish the same goal of severing the link between
politicians and lobbyists, as would more privatization. Although it is
not likely to happen, a flat tax would help, too as it would eliminate
all tax breaks. Following their party's sweep of the 1994
Congressional elections, the Republicans did reduce the number of
Congressional committees; they also abandoned the practice of refer-
ring bills to more than one committee; and they cut congressional
staffs. Furthermore, they promised more changes in how Congress
conducts its business.

Congressional term limits—(which passed in 14 states in the
1992 elections, placing 156 house members and 30 senators under
limits—is the mechanism many hope will turn elected officials back
to governing. In 1994 seven more states voted in favor of term limits,

bringing the total to 22 states. Republican leaders have promised to propose a Federal Constitutional Amendment to impose term limits on all members of Congress. But there is already a term limit on the Presidency, and we now witness a President who has become a permanent candidate—someone whose sole preoccupation seems to be to "crawl through to reelection," as Bill Clinton himself is said to have aptly phrased it (Woodward, 1994, p. 165).

Candidate Clinton promised a politics of inclusion—a politics that would bring all groups into equal participation in the political process: environmentalists, homosexuals, feminists, Afro-Americans, all ethnic minorities, the homeless, the abortionists, not to mention the poor, the middle class, the elderly, and any group who had been alienated by the Reagan-Bush administrations. Then, President Clinton discovered that inclusion can lead to implosion. To satisfy any one group—for example the gays—can only lead to angering other groups. Quickly. At the end of April 1993, after less than four months in office, the *New York Times* reported that White House officials were "fuming" because interest groups who had helped to elect Mr. Clinton "will not practice more patience" (April 25, 1993).

As early as May 1993, computer-generated opinion polls revealed a marked decline in support for the Clinton administration, making the administration more risk-aversive—evidenced in procrastination, dithering, flip flops, and retreats on many policies and issues. So, after a mere 100 days in office, President Clinton, guided by the computer-generated polls, abandoned governing, forsaking it for campaigning across the country—campaigning, as the press put it, for his economic program, for his health care program, for his crime bill—or, as others put it, for reelection.

The crisis continues.

CONCLUSION
THE SPELL OF DESCARTES

On the 10th of November in the year 1619, Rene Descartes had a dream. In that dream, the Angel of Truth told him that the world is fundamentally mathematical in structure, that the laws of mathematics are the key to the mysteries of nature. Thus inspired, Descartes proceeded to combine analysis and geometry to create analytical geometry, the mathematics of spatial relations. Turning thereafter to specific problems in physics, he composed *Traite du Monde (Treatise of the World)*, a mathematical explanation of how the physical world works. The condemnation of Galileo gave him second thoughts about publishing his revolutionary new ideas, so the book did not appear in print until 1664, after his death. He did present the main outlines of his philosophy of nature in 1644 in the *Principles of Philosophy*, which explained all of the phenomena of nature in terms of particles—their magnitude, their motion, and the figures they composed.

Descartes's philosophy of science was wrong. Yet, the dream of Descartes lingered on. The dream that the world is fundamentally mathematical in structure became the basis for modern rationalism: the notion that the (trained) human mind is capable of understanding the universe we live in and capable of understanding all the goings-on in that universe. Rationalism, in turn, gave birth to the belief that humans so-enlightened could then create a civilization or culture that would function in accord with those rational (mathematical) principles the human mind had discovered. Thus, modern rationalism ushered in a period of unlimited optimism that human intelligence—if enlightened—could construct a better, if not a perfect, civilization or culture. Out of this came the belief in continual progress.

Yet, when the computer came along in the second half of the 20th century and made it possible to fulfill the dream of Descartes by encoding all of human culture in mathematics, the result was a deep cultural pessimism, a disillusion and despair about our social, political, economic, and intellectual condition.

What happened, as I have tried to show, is that the mathematization of culture that the computer made possible revealed risks in our social, political, economic, and intellectual worlds that we had not perceived before. Moreover, the mathematical exactitude of the risks calculated by the computer conferred on them a certainty that, understandably, generated widespread risk aversion everywhere.

Underlying this proclivity to avert risks is the ideology of egalitarianism. Egalitarianism maintains that whenever and wherever any person or group is at more risk than others, or at less risk than others, then the system is at fault—that is, the existing social, political, and economic arrangements are failing to protect everyone equally.

Thus, the ideology of egalitarianism both disposes people to become risk conscious and supplies an explanation of why such risks exist. Moreover, egalitarianism provides a blueprint for action: change the system—radically and totally—in order to create an ideal society, that is, an egalitarian society.

As I tried to show in Part One, the current widespread subscription to the ideology of egalitarianism grew out of the intellectual outlook of postmodernism, which has been propagated in colleges and universities by many philosophers, historians, literary critics and anthropologists since the 1960s. At the heart of postmodernism is epistemological relativism which asserts that since we can never demonstrate any proposition to be true, then all propositions have equal epistemic standing—none are privileged. With epistemological relativism all knowledge becomes subjective, and each community decides what is certain—for itself.

As I see it, the introduction of the computer into academic studies hastened the growth of epistemological relativism in the humanities and in the social sciences. Scholars expected the computer to help them attain a mathematical certitude never before possible. But attempts to use the computer in the humanities and in the social sciences brought forth attacks from those scholars who resented the attempt to mathematize their fields. Some of those who resisted mathematization adopted the stance of epistemological relativism, which derailed the computer movement by denying that any interpretation or theory—about a literary work, or about societies past or present—could be proven to be true, even by mathematical computation. If no theory or no interpretation was privileged, then scholars were free to put forth *any* theory, *any* interpretation. And they can do so with impunity, since under the tent of epistemological relativism every theory or interpretation is immunized against criticism. By expunging criticism and the critical tradition, these postmodern scholars undermined the growth of knowledge.

It is a short step from epistemological relativism to ethical relativism, which holds that no person, or group of persons, and no kind of conduct should be privileged. In the pre-postmodern world—that is, the modern world, which began winding down in the 1960s—those with power—white, Anglo-Saxon, males—were privileged: They dictated what conduct was correct, and they controlled the rest of society by dictating how they ought to behave. In doing this they secured their own interests by put everyone else at risk—socially, economically, and politically. To combat this hegemony of the powerful, to have a world where no one is at more, or less risk than another, we have moved toward a more egalitarian society.

In Part Two I tried to show how the coming of the computer heightened people's awareness of hitherto unknown and unrecognized threats to the environment, threats to human health and safety, and threats to the well-being of minority groups. To avert these risks our egalitarian-disposed society has created a climate of prevention that curtails and sometimes prohibits conduct that has the potential to endanger any creature's well-being. In such a climate people must behave so as not to put others at risk. This, I maintain, curtails the growth of the society.

In the economic realm, as I have tried to show in Part Three, the computer expanded and accelerated entrepreneurial activity. But at the same time the computer created massive job dislocation, making many workers risk aversive. By blaming these job dislocations on the new entrepreneurship, egalitarians succeeded in securing legislation that regulated and controlled risky economic activities. This curtailed economic growth.

In the political realm, as I have tried to show in Part Four, the coming of the computer has made politicians painfully aware that the pursuit of the public interest (governing) can endanger their own reelection. To avert the risk of not being reelected, many politicians have given up governing and have instead become permanent candidates. This has precipitated a crisis of democracy that threatens continued political growth.

Risk aversion curtails growth because it discourages experimentation—by which I mean the continual engagement in trial and error elimination. If politicians and entrepreneurs are too cautious to launch new trials—new policies or new enterprises—then neither political nor economic growth can take place. If scholars cease criticizing the content of the theories of one another, then errors will not be eliminated and knowledge will not advance. And if everyone in the society conforms to what is deemed to be the correct behavior, there will be less freedom in the society—less freedom to innovate, less freedom to criticize. Without freedom to experiment, society will stop growing.

Without continual trial and error elimination our social, political, and economic arrangements lose their flexibility. Paralyzed by risk aversion they become dysfunctional. In government and in the market, too, old and obsolescent programs and products continue and are not replaced by better ones. In the academy and in society at large, outlandish theories and conduct go uncriticized—so long as they are politically correct, that is, do not create risks to our health or safety, or to the environment, or to any minority group.

But the computer did more than heighten risk aversion. It brought a deeper message. The mathematization of the world the computer made possible has revealed that the world is more complex than we ever imagined. The computer has made us aware of how ignorant we are. We not only do not understand the physical world -- a world we did not create—we also do not understand the political, economic, and social worlds we have created. Descartes's dream was based on the assumption that humans could attain certainty, mathematical certainty, which would then enable us to build a better, if not a perfect, world. But when the computer enabled us to mathematize our culture, we began to realize that we do not understand, and *cannot* understand, what we have wrought.

Thus, the introduction of the computer into the humanities and the social sciences brought home the realization that there is no way to justify any theory or any interpretation as true. In addition, the use of the computer in the study of social phenomena not only revealed that our present social arrangements cause more dangers and more illness than we had ever realized, it also made clear that we never really know what we are doing—we can never anticipate all the possible health and environmental consequences of our actions. And, in the realm of politics, the applications of the computer increased the awareness by politicians that whatever they did, however they voted, they would antagonize some portion of their constituencies; even more dismaying, no politician could tell in advance which groups would be adversely affected. And, finally, in the economic realm, the coming of the computer revealed that certainty was beyond the grasp of those who "truck, barter, and exchange": We cannot plan, control, or anticipate the outcomes of our economic transactions.

All this indicates that Descartes's dream was naught but a dream, that modern rationalism is bankrupt, and that the enlightenment was a misguided project.

Yet, the spell of Descartes is broad and deep. From his time to our own, most people have shared the view that the accumulation of knowledge and the application of the scientific method will enable us to bring our social, political, and economic arrangements under control and thereby serve the public interest. We persist in believing that fallible human beings, in John Donne's words, can "grasp this sorry scheme entire and remold it to our heart's desire."

But, if human beings are fallible, as most people will readily admit—and as the computer has clearly confirmed—then certainty is not ours to be had. So, the quest for certainty, a quest that has dominated western philosophy from Descartes to Wittgenstein, seems not to be the path through which we can improve our culture. Yet, if humans are fallible, if certainty is not to be had, then how can we explain the fact, and it *is* a fact, that things have gotten better since the time of Descartes? There is more wealth, greater safety and health, increased freedom and equality, and considerable advancement in knowledge since the 17th century. How did these improvements come about?

Not as Descartes envisioned. Not by obtaining knowledge that was certain and then applying that knowledge, as the myth of modern rationalism would have it. Rather, such improvements as we have secured have come about, I suggest, as the result of criticism. I maintain that we have, over time, through criticism, uncovered inadequacies in our existing culture, and then improved that culture by diminishing or reducing those uncovered inadequacies.

This has happened with our social arrangements—think of the practices once accepted that we have eliminated since the time of Descartes: slavery, child labor, witch-burning, racial segregation. We have done this with our political arrangements—think of the actions taken to eliminate tyranny, secure rights, and insure the peaceful change of governments, as well as actions taken to combat poverty and disenfranchisement. We have done this in our economic arrangements—think of how we have eliminated inefficient methods of production, marketing, distribution, and merchandising. And we have done this in the intellectual world, too—think of the myths we have debunked, the erroneous theories we have refuted, and the ignorance we have liquidated.

Although it is through the critical approach that we have actually improved our culture, many people remain under the spell of Descartes, believing that we must first have an idea or understanding of what a perfect or good culture is before we can improve what exists. This belief denies, or attempts to transcend, our condition of human fallibility. For, since we are fallible, we cannot ever come up with an idea or conception of a perfect polity, a perfect society, or a perfect economy.

We can, however, improve our culture by criticizing what already exists: by looking for what is wrong, inadequate, harmful, mistaken, in what already exists. Media of communication—like television and computers (and the printing press and writing)—facilitate this criticism by encoding the culture in pictures, or in mathematics (or in words on a page). Media of communication "objectify" the culture, distancing it from us, so that we can better criticize it. It is important to note that we do not have to know what a good polity, economy, or society is—nor even what a correct policy, practice or procedure would be—in order to ascertain that the existing one is inadequate—as every mathematician, scientist, cook, engineer, and painter knows.

The criticism I speak of has taken place through institutions. The market, for example, is an institution that facilitates economic criticism—the criticism of the quality of goods, as well as the price of goods. As a result, the market has helped to improve the quality of goods as well as their distribution. Through the criticisms of consumers and competitors that the market encourages and channels, wealth has increased enormously since the 17th century.

In the same way, our constitutional institutions have facilitated and channeled political criticism. Through the separation of governmental powers and checks and balances, as well as through the party system, frequent elections, a written constitution, a bill of rights, and other political institutions, we have been able to criticize and modify or eliminate existing laws and policies that have limited freedom or curtailed equality, thereby improving the polity.

And in the intellectual world, the community of scholars—an institution held together and operating through the media of writing, print, and oral discussion—has facilitated and dispersed criticisms of theories and ideas, thereby advancing knowledge in all fields and disciplines.

Finally, our social institutions—our families, churches, philanthropic foundations, voluntary societies, and organizations—have always criticized social conduct that is harmful to our health, safety, and well-being.

None of these institutions—political, social, economic, or intellectual—were consciously designed: They evolved. They evolved as cultural mechanisms through which people can protect themselves: protect themselves against tyrannical and arbitrary political leaders, protect themselves against fraudulent and deceptive economic entrepreneurs, protect themselves against threats to their health and safety, and protect themselves against false theories and erroneous ideas. Moreover, all these institutions can be traced back to antiquity—although all were significantly strengthened by the introduction of the printing press in the late 15th century. It was largely through the help of the printing press, as I have argued elsewhere, that we have been able to construct constitutional governments, a market economy, an open society, and a community of scholars (Perkinson, 1995).

If I am correct about how culture gets better and continues to get better, then such improvements as we have already secured have always come about indirectly and in a negative way: through the elimination or reduction of bads and evils that criticism has uncovered. In their efforts to protect themselves and their own well-being, people have acted as critical citizens, critical consumers, critical workers, and critical scholars. By being critical we have reduced the inadequacies, the bads, and the evils in our culture.

So, the fundamental danger in the present widespread aversion to risk is that risk itself is viewed as bad, as an evil to be eliminated. Risk, however, comes with the human condition; risk inheres in every human endeavor and every project: our laws, theories, enterprises, and diurnal social activities all entail risk. As fallible beings we can never know fully the consequences of our actions, nor the implications of our theories. We never know what we are doing; nor—because we can never know all the implications of our thoughts—do we ever understand what we are thinking. So, if we accept our human fallibility, then we must accept risk and risk taking as part of the human condition.

Philosophers from Descartes to Wittgenstein have tried to show us how to escape this condition of human fallibility, how to attain certainty. To no avail. Yet the spell of Descartes continues. And when the computer provides such mathematical certainty about risks, many caught in that spell conclude that such certainty could enable us to avert risks by making dramatic changes in our political, social, and economic institutions.

But our efforts to avert risks may destroy the very institutions that have, so far, brought about improvement in our culture. For, as I have tried to show in this book, many of the actions recently taken to avert risk have weakened the free market, circumvented representative democratic government, threatened the open society, and debilitated the community of scholars. As these institutions decline, criticism is curtailed, improvement falters, and our despair about our culture deepens and darkens.

Yet, all this happens only because we still remain under the spell of Descartes. That is, we still continue to try to create a rational culture based on knowledge we know to be certain. So, because we still believe it possible to know what we are doing, and believe it possible to foresee the effects of our actions, we therefore see risks as something to avoid, something to eliminate. And now that the computer has made us more aware of risks we have, as a consequence, become a risk-aversive culture.

However, this increased awareness of risks need not lead us to risk aversion. Instead, it can lead to conscious and deliberate risk taking. For the increased awareness of risks the computer has made possible points out some of the specific limits of human knowledge, thereby reaffirming risk taking as one of the burdens of civilization. Without risks, there can be no growth, no progress—no economic or intellectual growth, no political or social progress.

So, if we are to continue to grow, to improve, to get better, then the task before us is not to avert risk but rather to experiment, to engage in trial and error elimination. But we can continue to experiment only if we maintain and strengthen those traditional institutions and arrangements that have enabled critical citizens, critical consumers, critical scholars, and critical workers to protect themselves. As long as these traditional arrangements keep criticism alive so that we can protect ourselves, we can encourage politicians, entrepreneurs, and scholars to take risks—not to try to avert them.

REFERENCES

Abrahamson, Jeffrey, F. Christopher Arterton, and Gary Orren. *The Electronic Commonwealth*. New York: Basic Books, 1988.

Adams, Walter, and James W. Brock. *Dangerous Pursuits*. New York: Pantheon Books, 1989.

Anderson, Walter Truett. *Reality is Not What it Used to Be*. New York: Harper and Row, 1990.

Aronson, Sidney. *Status and Kinship in the Higher Civil Service*. Cambridge: Harvard University Press, 1964.

Balling, Robert C. *The Heated Debate: Greenhouse Predictions Versus Climate Reality*. San Francisco: Pacific Research Institute for Public Policy, 1992.

Bartlett, Donald L., and James B. Steele. *America: What Went Wrong?* Kansas City: Andrews and McMeel, 1992.

Bartley, Robert L. *The Seven Fat Years*. New York: The Free Press, 1992.

Bartley, William W., III. *Wittgenstein*. LaSalle, IL: Open Court, 1973.

_____. *Unfathomed Knowledge, Unmeasured Wealth*. LaSalle, IL: Open Court, 1990.

Beal, Richard S, and Ronald H. Hinckley. "Decision Making and Opinion Polls." *The Annals of the American Academy of Political and Social Science*, March 1984.

Beniger, James R. *The Control Revolution*. Cambridge: Harvard University Press, 1986.

Benson, Lee. *The Concept of Jacksonian Democracy*. Princeton: Princeton University Press, 1961.

Blanchard, Brand (ed.). *Education in the Age of Science*. New York: Basic Books, 1959.

Bloom, Allan. *The Closing of the American Mind*. New York: Simon and Schuster, 1987.

Blume, Marshall, Jeremy Siegel, and Dan Rottenberg. *Revolution on Wall Street*. New York: Norton, 1993.

Bolgar, R.R. *The Classical Heritage and its Beneficiaries*. New York: Harper & Row, 1964.

Boren, David. "Why I Am Leaving the Senate." *New York Times*, May 13, 1994.

Bori, G. "The Regulation of Carcinogenic Hazards." *Science, 208*, 1980.

Bovard, James. *Lost Rights*. New York: St. Martin's Press, 1994.

Bridenbaugh, Carl. "The Great Mutation." *American Historical Review*, January 1984.

Brzezinski, Zbigniew. *Two Ages: America's Role in the Technetronic Era*. New York: The Viking Press, 1970.

Burrows, J.F. *Computation into Criticism*. New York: Oxford University Press, 1987.

Carnap, Rudolph. *The Logical Structure of the Physical World*. Berkeley: University of California Press, 1967. (Original date of publication 1929)

Carson, Rachel. *The Silent Spring*. Boston: Houghton Mifflin Company, 1962.

Chudacuff, Howard P. *How Old Are You?* Princeton: Princeton University Press, 1989.

Clarke, William C. "Witches, Floods, and Wonder Drugs: Historical Perspectives on Risk Management." In *Societal Risk Assessment* (eds. Richard Schwing and Walter Albers). New York: Plenum Press, 1980.

Commoner, Barry. *The Closing Circle*. New York: Alfred A. Knopf, 1971.

Covello, Vincent T. Risk *Evaluation and Management*. New York: Plenum Press, 1986.

Crespi, Irving. *Public Opinion, Polls, and Democracy*. Boulder, Colorado: Westview Press, 1988.

Crews, Frederick. *Sceptical Engagements*. New York: Oxford University Press, 1986.

Crossen, Cynthia. *Tainted Truth: The Manipulation of Fact in America*. New York: Simon and Schuster, 1994.

Davis, Natalie Z. *Society and Culture in Early Modern France*. Stanford: Stanford University Press, 1975.

Dionne, E.J. *Why Americans Hate Politics*. New York: Simon and Schuster, 1991.

Douglas, Mary and Aaron Wildavsky. *Risk and Culture*. Berkeley: University of California Press, 1982.

Economic Report of the President, 1991. Washington, DC: U.S. Government Printing Office, 1991.

Edsall, Thomas Byrne with Mary Edsall. *Chain Reaction*. New York: Norton, 1991.

Ehrlich Paul. *The Population Bomb*. New York: Ballantine Books, 1968.

Engelman, Paul. *Letters from Ludwig Wittgenstein*. Oxford: Basil Blackwell, 1967.

Erikson, Robert, Norman Luttberg, and Kent Tedin. *American Public Opinion*. New York: John Wiley and Sons, 1980.

Fish, Stanley. "What is Stylistics and Why Are They Saying Such Terrible Things About It"? In *Approaches to Poetics* (ed. Seymour Chatman). New York: Columbia University Press, 1973.

_____. *Doing What Comes Naturally*. Durham, NC: Duke University Press, 1989.

Fogel, Robert W. and G.R. Elton. *Which Road to the Past?* New Haven: Yale University Press, 1983.

Fogel, Robert W. and Stanley Engelman. *Time on the Cross: The Economics of American Slavery*. Boston: Little Brown, 1974.

Gans, Herbert. *People, Places and Policies*. New York: Columbia University Press, 1991.

Geertz, Clifford. *The Interpretation of Cultures*. New York: Basic Books, 1973.

_____. *Local Knowledge*. New York: Basic Books, 1983.

Gilder, George. *The Spirit of Enterprise*. New York: Simon and Schuster, 1984.

Ginsberg, Benjamin and Martin Shefter. *Politics By Other Means*. New York: Basic Books, 1990.

Global 2000 Report to the President. New York: Penguin Books, 1992.

Gould, Stephen Jay. *The Mismeasure of Man*. New York: Norton, 1981.

Greider, William. *Who Will Tell the People? The Betrayal of American Democracy*. New York: Simon and Schuster, 1992.

Grenier, Richard. *Capturing the Culture*. Washington, DC: Ethics and Public Policy Center, 1991.

Greve, Michael S. and Fred L. Smith Jr. (eds). *Environmental Politics*. New York: Praeger, 1992.

Gross, Paul R. and Norman Levitt. *Higher Superstition*. Baltimore: Johns Hopkins University Press, 1994.

Guinier, Lani. *The Tyranny of the Majority*. New York: The Free Press, 1994.

Hacker, Andrew. *U/S: A Statistical Portrait of the American People*. New York: The Viking Press, 1983.

_____. *Two Nations*. New York: Charles Scribner's Sons, 1992.

Hamrin, Robert. *America's New Economy*. New York: Franklin Watts, 1988.

Handlin, Oscar. *Truth in History*. Cambridge: Harvard University Press, 1979.

Hartz, Louis. *The Liberal Tradition in America*. New York: Harper & Row, 1955.

Hentoff, Nat. *Free Speech for Me—But Not for Thee*. New York: Harper Collins, 1992.

Himmelfarb, Gertrude. *On Looking into the Abyss*. New York: Alfred A. Knopf, 1994.

Huber, Peter. *Liability*. New York: Basic Books, 1988.

Innes, Judith E. *Knowledge and Public Policy: The Search for Meaningful Indicators*. New Brunswick: Transaction Publishers, 1990.

Iser, Wolfgang. *The Act of Reading: A Theory of Aesthetic Response*. Baltimore: Johns Hopkins University Press.

Jameson, Frederic. *The Prison House of Language*. Princeton: Princeton University Press, 1972.

Kammen, Michael. *The Past Before Us*. Ithaca, NY: Cornell University Press, 1980.

Kernan, Alvin. *The Death of Literature*. New Haven: Yale University Press, 1990.

Kimball, Roger. *Tenured Radicals*. New York: Harper and Row, 1990.

King, Mary. *The Great American Banking Snafu*. Lexington, MA: Lexington Books, 1985.

Kirk, Marshall and Hunter Madsen. *After the Ball*. Garden City, NY: Doubleday, 1989.

Kirkland, Edward. Review of Robert Fogel, *Railroads and American Economic Growth*. In *American Historical Review*, July 1967.

Kline, Morris. *Mathematics in Western Culture*. New York: Oxford University Press, 1953.

Krugman, Paul. *Peddling Prosperity*. New York: Norton, 1994.

Kuhn, Thomas. *The Structure of Scientific Revolutions*. Chicago: The University of Chicago Press, 1970. (Original date of publication 1962)

Kuhn, Thomas. *The Essential Tension*. Chicago: University of Chicago Press, 1977.

Landes, David S. and Charles Tilly. *History as Social Science*. Englewood Cliffs: Prentice-Hall, 1971.

Landy, Marc K. and Mary Hague. "Private Interests and Superfund." *The Public Interest*, Summer 1992.

Laumann, Edward O., John H. Gagnon, Robert T. Michael and Stuart Michaels. *The Social Organization of Sexuality: Sexual Practices in The United States*. Chicago: The University of Chicago Press, 1994.

Lekachman, Robert. *Greed is Not Enough*. New York: Pantheon Books, 1982.

Le Roy Ladurie, Emmanuel. *The Peasants of Languedoc.* Campaign: University of Illinois Press, 1977.

Levi-Strauss, Claude. *Structural Anthropology.* New York: Basic Books, 1963.

Lindsey, Lawrence. *The Growth Experiment.* New York: Basic Books, 1990.

Lippman, Walter. *Public Opinion.* New York: Harcourt, Brace and Company, 1922.

McKenzie, Richard B. and Dwight R. Lee. *Quicksilver Capital.* New p;York: The Free Press, 1991.

MacKinnon, Catherine A. *Only Words.* Cambridge: Harvard University Press, 1993.

Magnet, Myron. *The Dream and the Nightmare.* New York: William Morrow and Company, 1993.

Malbin, Michael J. *Unelected Representatives.* New York: Basic Books, 1980.

Marrou, H.I. *A History of Education in Antiquity.* New York: Sheed and Ward, 1956.

May, Henry. *The Enlightenment in America.* New York: Oxford University Press, 1976.

Mayer, Martin. *The Money Bazaars.* New York: E.P. Dutton, 1984.

Meadows, Donnella, Dennis Meadows, Jorgen Randers, and William Behren, III. *The Limits to Growth.* New York: The New American Library, 1972.

Morone, James A. *The Democratic Wish.* New York: Basic Books, 1990.

Myrdal, Gunnar. *Against the Stream: Critical Essays on Economics.* New York: Vintage Books, 1975.

_____. "Economics of an Improved Environment." In *Who Speaks for Earth?* (ed. Maurice F. Strong). New York: Norton, 1973.

Nie, Norman H., Sidney Verba, and John Petrocik. *The Changing American Voter.* Cambridge: Harvard University Press, 1979.

Olson, Walter K. *The Litigation Explosion.* New York: Truman Talley, 1981.

Overing, Joanna (ed.) *Reason and Morality.* London: Tavistock Publishers, 1985.

Perkinson, Henry J. *Getting Better: Television and Moral Progress.* New Brunswick, NJ: Transaction Publishers, 1991.

_____. *How Things Got Better: Speech, Writing, Printing, and Cultural Change.* Westport, CT: Bergin and Garvey, 1995.

Phillips, Kevin. *Boiling Point.* New York: Random House, 1993.

Potter, Rosanne G. (ed.). *Literary Computing and Literary Criticism.* Philadelphia: University of Pennsylvania Press, 1989.

Quellette, Lydia Thomas, Edward Mangold, and Paul Cheremisinoff. *Automation Impacts Industry.* Ann Arbor: Ann Arbor Science Publishers, 1983.

Rabb, Theodore K. *The New History*. Princeton: Princeton University Press, 1982.

Rauch, Jonathan. *Demosclerosis*. New York: Times Books, 1994.

Ray, Dixie Lee. *Trashing the Planet*. Washington, DC: Regnery Gateway, 1990.

_____. *Environmental Overkill*. Washington, DC: Regnery Gateway, 1993.

Reich, Robert B. *The Work of Nations*. New York: Alfred A. Knopf, 1991.

Reiser, Stanley Joel. *Medicine and the Reign of Technology*. New York: Cambridge University Press, 1978.

Roberts, Sam. *Who We Are: A Portrait of America Based on the Latest U.S. Census*. New York: Times Books, 1993.

Robinson, Edward J. "Analyzing the Impact of Science Reporting." *Journalism Quarterly*, Summer 1963.

Robinson, John P. and John A. Fleishman. "Ideological Trends in American Public Opinion." *The Annals of the American Academy of Political and Social Sciences*, March 1984.

Rorty, Richard. *Philosophy and the Mirror of Nature*. Princeton: Princeton University Press, 1979.

_____. *Consequences of Pragmatism*. Minneapolis: University of Minnesota Press, 1982.

_____. *Essays on Heidegger and Others* (Vol. 2). Cambridge: Cambridge University Press, 1991.

Rubenstein, Edwin. *The Right Data*. New York: National Review, 1994.

Shaw, Peter. *The War Against Intellect*. Iowa City: University of Iowa Press, 1989.

Simon, Julian L. *The Ultimate Resource*. Princeton: Princeton University Press, 1981.

Smith, Hedrick. *The Power Game: How Washington Works*. New York: Random House, 1988.

Sorauf, Frank J. *Money in American Culture*. Glenview, IL: Scott, Foresman and Company, 1988.

Starr, Chauncey. "Social Benefit Versus Technological Risk: What is Our Society Willing to Pay for Safety?" *Science, 165* (September 19, 1969), 1232-1238.

Stewart, James B. *Den of Thieves*. New York: Simon and Schuster, 1991.

Stockman, David. *The Triumph of Politics*. New York: Harper and Row, 1986.

Surgeon General's Report on Nutrition and Health, 1988. Rocklin, CA: Prima Publishing and Communications, 1989.

Sussman, Barry. *What Americans Really Think*. New York: Pantheon Books, 1988.

Sykes, Charles J. *The Hollow Men: Politics and Corruption in Higher Education*. Washington, DC: Regnery Gateway, 1990.

_____. *A Nation of Victims*. New York: St. Martin's Press, 1992.

Taylor, Jared. *Paved with Good Intentions*. New York: Carroll and Graf Publishers, 1992.

Thernstrom, Stephen. "Quantitative Methods in History: Some Notes." In *Sociology and History: Methods* (eds. Seymour Lipset and Richard Hofstadter). New York: Basic Books, 1968.

_____. *The Other Bostonians: Poverty and Progress in the Human Metropolis*. Cambridge: Harvard University Press, 1973.

Tilly, Charles. *The Formation of National States in Western Europe*. Princeton: Princeton University Press, 1975.

Toffler, Alvin. *Powershift*. New York: Bantam Books, 1990.

Toqueville, Alexis de. *Democracy in America* (ed. Phillips Bradley). New York, Knopf, 1948.

Trimble, Vance H. *Sam Walton, Founder of Wal-Mart*. New York: Penguin, 1991.

Tyler, Stephen A. "Postmodern Ethnography: From Document of the Occult to Occult Document. In *Writing Culture* (eds. James Clifford and George E. Marcus). Berkeley: University of California Press, 1986.

U.S. President's Research Committee on Social Trends. *Recent Social Trends*. New York: McGraw-Hill, 1933.

Universal Almanac 1993. Kansas City, MO: Andrews and McMeel.

Vedder, Richard K. and Lowell E. Gallaway. *Out of Work*. New York: Holmes and Meier, 1993.

Veroff, Joseph, Elizabeth Douvan, and Richard A. Kulka. *The Inner American*. New York: Basic Books, 1981.

White, Douglas. "Mathematical Anthropology." In *Handbook of Social and Cultural Anthropology* (ed. John J. Honigmann). Chicago: Rand McNally, 1973.

White, Lawrence J. *The S&L Debacle* New York: Oxford University Press, 1991.

Wildavsky, Aaron. "No Risk is the Highest Risk of All." In *Readings in Risk* (eds. Theodore Glickman and Robert Gough). Washington, DC: Resources for the Future, 1990.

_____. *The Rise of Radical Egalitarianism*. Washington, DC: The American University Press, 1991.

Will, George F. *Restoration: Congress, Term Limits and the Recovery of Deliberative Democracy*. New York: The Free Press, 1992.

Wittgenstein, Ludwig. *Philosophical Investigations*. Oxford: Basil Blackwell, 1958.

_____. *Tractatus Logico Philosophicus*. New York: Humanities Press, 1961. (Original date of publication 1922).

_____. *On Certainty*. New York: Harper and Row, 1969.

Wolf, Charles Jr. "The New Mercantilism." *The Public Interest*, Summer 1994.

Wolpe, Bruce C. *Lobbying Congress*. Washington DC: Congressional Quarterly Press, 1990.

Woodward, Bob. *The Agenda*. New York: Simon and Schuster, 1994.

Wright, Gordon. "History of a Moral Science." *American Historical Review*, January 1976.

Yago, Glenn. *Junk Bonds*. New York: Oxford University Press, 1991.

Yardley, Jonathan. "Clean Fuels, Dirty Air: How a (Bad) Bill Became Law." *The Public Interest*, Summer 1992.

Zinn, Howard. *The Politics of History*. Boston: Beacon Press, 1970.

Zuboff, Shoshana. *In the Age of the Smart Machine*. New York: Basic Books, 1984.

INDEX